FREEDOM AND RE

FREEDOM AND RESPONSIBILITY

A Search for Harmony – Human Rights and Personal Dignity

Selected addresses by
His Holiness Kirill, Patriarch of Moscow and All Russia

with Appendix:
The Russian Orthodox Church's Basic Teaching on Human Dignity,
Freedom and Rights, published by the Bishops' Council of the Russian
Orthodox Church in June 2008

Foreword by The Rt Revd and Rt Hon Richard Chartres,
Bishop of London

DARTON · LONGMAN + TODD

Publishing House of
the Moscow Patriarchate

First published in 2011 by
Darton, Longman and Todd Ltd
1 Spencer Court
140 – 142 Wandsworth High Street
London SW18 4JJ

Original Russian text Свобода и ответственность: в поисках гармонии.
Права человека и достоинство личности, Moscow 2008,

Translations by Deacons Michael Lomax and Basil Bush and the Department
for External Relations of the Moscow Patriarchate

*This work is published in partnership between Darton, Longman and Todd, London
and the Publishing House of the Moscow Patriarchate, Moscow, with the participation
of the Department of External Church Relations of the Moscow Patriarchate and
the St Gregory the Theologian Charity Foundation.*

ISBN: 978-0-232-52870-1 (paperback)
ISBN: 978-0-232-52879-4 (hardback)

Phototypeset by Kerrypress Ltd, Luton, Bedfordshire
Printed and bound in Great Britain by CPI Antony Rowe, Chippenham

CONTENTS

FOREWORD

Metropolitan Kirill, as he then was, visited London towards the end of the 1980s to give a lecture in the City of London. It was a time when there was still no clarity about how events in the Soviet Union would unfold. I remember the Metropolitan's translator saying in near despair, 'My job is so difficult these days. You never know what he is going to say next.'

With acute intelligence and wide experience of the western world, the Patriarch today leads a Church of more than seventy million believers. The social doctrine and the direction of travel of the Russian Orthodox Church is a matter of high significance for European culture as a whole.

The tragic experience of Russian Christians and especially of the Russian Orthodox Church in the twentieth century is both a warning and an inspiration. The homicidal philanthropy of the Revolution sought to build a heaven on earth on scientific principles. This involved from time to time the attempt to extirpate what was seen as the virus of religion.

Members of Patriarch Kirill's own family were among the millions of victims of this persecution but he speaks with an authentically modern voice to the world which was brought into being by the disintegration of the Soviet Empire.

In this collection of addresses and articles which were published in Russian over a twenty-five year period, the Patriarch poses the question of how the spiritual energy and resources of the Orthodox Tradition in particular can co-exist with and contribute to the peace and flourishing of a world in which many people see the great world religions either as nothing more than local editions of 'universal values' or even as breeding grounds for prejudice and conflict.

Is co-existence in economics, politics and in inter-governmental relations between liberal institutions and traditional communities possible? One answer is to collude with the privatisation of faith, as if becoming a Christian were a lifestyle choice on a par with opting for vegetarianism. It is an answer which the Patriarch emphatically rejects and he explores the basis on which Christians can as Christians participate in the political process.

It may be that the spirit-filled tradition of communities of faith will come to constitute the vital alchemy which transforms abstract principles into a habitable ethos. All too frequently, deprived of the spiritual energy which flows from the beauty of holy living in a community of love, the highest ideals can lie inert in solemn-sounding declarations and endless fidgeting with regulation.

The Patriarch writes in a way that will infuriate many of the high priests of 'universal values' but such provocation must be compatible with a genuinely liberal society. It is good that we now have an opportunity in English to appreciate the thinking of this significant protagonist of a 'multi-polar' world. An additional advantage of this collection is that the text of the Russian Orthodox Church's Basic Teaching on Human Dignity, Freedom and Rights is printed in the Appendix. First published in 2008, the Patriarch himself played a large part in its preparation and it repays careful study.

✠ Richard Londin

Chapter 1

RELIGIOUS FAITH AS THE SOURCE OF SOCIAL NORMS

Published in Tserkov i vremya, *no. 2, 1999, and in* Nezavisimaya Gazeta, *16–17 February 2000*

The most fundamental conflict of our present era is the clash between the liberal model of civilisation on the one hand and national cultural and religious identity on the other. For me it is the single largest challenge facing the human community in the twenty-first century. Research into the genesis of this opposition and the search for ways of overcoming it need to occupy an important place in Orthodox theological studies.

Resolving the conflict could play a major part in determining the future shape of human civilisation. This explains why the fact of raising this problem, and initial attempts to define it, arouse both genuine interest and genuine anger.

The anger comes from those who, from certain ideological positions, deny the very existence of such a problem; from those quarters that fear a revision or correction of the liberal ideas which underpin current attempts to form a new and global image of human community from the melting pot of civilisations and cultures. And no less anger comes from those zealots or religious and cultural fundamentalists who have long since resolved all these problems in their own minds, deeply convinced that the only road to salvation is to retreat behind tightly-bolted doors. Despite this, it is encouraging that many people, both in Russia and abroad, have expressed lively interest in further discussion of the relationship between liberal and traditional ideas and values.

Methodologically, and by the very nature of the problem, this discussion belongs not only to the realm of international relations and the need to create a just world order, but equally to that of the individual and of modern society in general. Resolution of this fundamental problem will also help answer a whole range of related problems of Church–society, inter-confessional and inter-religious relations.

Of course, a knowledge of the Church's teaching, personal experience of prayer, the ability to distinguish Orthodoxy from other denominations, an understanding of the historical roots and spiritual culture of their country and many other faith-related areas remain essential for an Orthodox man or woman in the twenty-first century. But the foremost priority must be to assimilate religion into life, into a lifestyle predicated on religious motivation. Modern society is constantly inculcating into people that religious faith is a purely private, indeed intimate affair of the human individual. In liberal, secularised societies, the only choices for which religious motivation is seen as permissible are those limited to a citizen's personal or, in extreme cases, family life. In other aspects of human existence there is no room, nor can there be, for religious motivation.

Personal ethics do indeed lie at the very heart of Christian morality. The Christian message is aimed in the first place at the individual person, seeking to elicit a personal spiritual experience and response which will open the way to the transfiguration of his or her soul. Nonetheless, these salvation-bringing changes in our inner worlds take place not in isolation from the external environment, not in special laboratory conditions, but in real and living contact with the people around us: in the first instance in our families, then with our colleagues at work, with society and, ultimately, with the institutions of State. It is not possible to be a Christian inside the walls of one's own home, in one's family circle or in the solitude of one's cell and to cease to be Christian when teaching at university or in school, standing in front of a television camera, voting in Parliament or undertaking a scientific experiment. Christian motivation must be present in everything that constitutes the believer's sphere of vital interests. A believer cannot exclude his professional life or scientific interests, his political, economic or social activities, his work in the media and the like from this spiritual and moral context. Religious belief encompasses everything a believer is or does. The religious way of life is the mode of existence in the world of people whose choices are motivated and determined by their religious principles.

The religious way of life – and in this case I am are talking of the Orthodox way of life – is distinguished by its rootedness in the tradition of the Church. For the Orthodox Christian, tradition is a set of creedal and moral truths that the Church has accepted from the testimony of the Apostles and which it has guarded and developed as a function of the historical circumstances and challenges facing it down the ages. Briefly, tradition is the living, grace-filled stream of the Church's faith and life. Tradition provides the norm by which the life of faith is necessarily and vitally governed. Every departure from tradition is therefore understood by the Orthodox as a violation of this norm of faith, or, put simply, as heresy.

It is the tradition of the Church that provides the criterion of whether a particular way of life is Orthodox or not. Rooted in it, it is Orthodox, outside it, it is not. Here, of course, we are talking not so much of the external manifestations of a faithfulness to tradition or of the cultural significance of tradition in the history of individuals and society. This rootedness in tradition is revealed in the values by which we live our lives. Only a life lived in accordance with tradition as normative for faith and behaviour may be regarded as truly Orthodox life.

Today, many of our countrymen face the challenge of not only assimilating and holding fast to the faith, but even more of assimilating and holding fast to the way of life defined by this faith. For the norm of faith to become the standard by which a person governs his life calls not only for knowledge about, but for real, first-hand experience of life in the Church. We have to be partakers of its Mystery. Only then will following the norm of faith be as natural as 'breath, glorifying the Lord'. Only then will it not become an 'unbearable yoke' or, worse, Pharisaism killing the very spirit of faith; but, like a blessed 'covering mantle', it will protect the believer throughout his life. Adherence to this norm does not constrain or limit or violate human freedom. Rather it protects it from destruction, just as the mother's womb protects the life evolving in it.

Maintaining this norm and affirming it in modern society as a vital, ontological value is the task of every intelligent member of the Church. It is also, more specifically, the task of contemporary theology. This norm is as strong as it is fragile. As the experience of individual lives and entire communities demonstrates, it can be damaged or even destroyed. It can also be preserved and strengthened by contact with different cultural and civilisational standards, with other norms of life. We come into contact with such 'otherness' when, for example, we live side by side with people of other views and convictions, bearing other cultural and civilisational codes.

To these I will now turn my attention. In most cases where other ways of life are based on their own traditions, they do not represent any danger to Orthodox values. Orthodox have in Russia lived side by side and interacted for centuries with Muslims, Jews, Buddhists and certain other Christian denominations. Throughout the history of our country such religious–cultural intersection has almost never taken on a destructive character. In the context of Russian civilisation, the various rules, standards and traditions of each group more often than not did not conflict with, but rather supported one another. And for this reason Russian Orthodox people have always lived peacefully with foreigners and peoples of other faiths. The only exceptions have been where an alien faith and alien standards of life have been imposed on our people by force or by proselytism. Then the people have risen up to defend their faith and the lifestyle that they perceived as the norm and under threat of destruction. Typically, this has been due to foreign aggression. And for this reason our whole history is marked by the struggle, not only to preserve our national and political independence, but also to maintain the tradition of our fatherland, the norm of faith and its associated form of life. However, in the absence of such attacks on their religious and cultural identity, Russians' coexistence with bearers of other civilisational standards has proved remarkably harmonious.

Orthodox people have interacted with interest, curiosity and often genuine respect with foreigners and non-Orthodox, paying tribute in particular to their professional and military skills. They have frequently adopted foreign cultural realities, social skills and working methods. It may be precisely because of what Dostoevsky called the Russian people's 'responsiveness to the whole world' that our land has not been watered with the blood of religious wars. Rather, we can speak of the formation, far back in Russian history, of a model of peaceful coexistence of various religious codes and lifestyles, each rooted in its own tradition and each having its own clearly defined – and therefore well-known to each other – value systems. The fact that Muslims and Jews fought side by side with Orthodox in the Russian army to defend their common homeland is a visible embodiment of such mutual respect for each others' religious and cultural experience and an implicit rejection of any desire to impose one's own way of life on one's neighbour.

The rapid development of communications and mass media in modern times has radically changed not only the face of the world, but also the structure of inter-personal, inter-ethnic and inter-state relations. In today's world almost all the boundaries that formerly separated national cultures have come tumbling down. Today people move with unprecedented ease right around the globe, freely choosing to live and work anywhere in the world. This is producing enormous cultural and ethnic displacements, the full consequences of which we have not yet fully grasped. The era of mono-ethnic and mono-confessional states is gradually disappearing before our very eyes. For example, the Muslim presence on the European continent is a socio-cultural factor that can not be ignored. The world has become open, diffuse, inter-penetrating. How should individuals and human communities respond to this challenge?

As the historical experience of Russia witnesses, contact and mutual influence between religious and cultural traditions may, under certain conditions (rejection of proselytism, aggression, etc.) be not only harmless for the conservation of cultural and religious identity, but also mutually enriching.

The real problem lies elsewhere, in the absence of barriers in today's world to protect nations' spiritual health and their religious and historical identity from the expansion of alien, destructive social and cultural factors; from the new way of life that is arising and taking shape outside of any tradition under the influence of today's post-industrial world. At the basis of this lifestyle are liberal ideas, combining pagan anthropocentrism – which entered European culture through the Renaissance – Protestant theology and Jewish philosophical thought. By the end of the Enlightenment these ideas had shaped themselves into a certain set of liberal principles. The French Revolution marked the culmination of this spiritual and ideological revolution, based on the rejection of the normative significance of tradition. Where did this revolution start? With the Reformation and with the reformers' rejection of the normative significance of tradition in the field of Christian dogma. In Protestantism, tradition ceased being a criterion of truth, to be replaced by the believer's personal understanding of the Scriptures and personal religious experience. Protestantism is in essence a liberal reading of Christianity.

Allow me to add in passing that the current crisis of ecumenism is in the first instance a methodological crisis. Why? Because, at the start of inter-confessional dialogue, instead of attempting to agree on the most important thing (that is, an understanding of Holy Tradition as normative for Christian faith and practice and a criterion of theological truth), Christians began to discuss individual questions, however important these may be in themselves. The manifest success in the discussion of these questions is really almost irrelevant, because what meaning can doctrinal agreement have when one party (a significant portion of Protestant theologians) does not recognise the very concept of normativity for Christian faith and practice? Any agreement in these fields is open to withdrawal or revision when new ideas and new arguments appear, introducing new seeds of division. Is not this the phenomenon we are facing today with the problem of women's priesthood and acceptance of homosexual lifestyles? Apropos, the histories of women's priesthood and of homosexuality are the best proofs of the thesis on the liberal nature of Protestantism. It is very clear that the introduction of women's priesthood and acceptance of homosexual lifestyles occurred under the influence of the liberal idea of human rights. In the case in point, these rights represent a radical departure from Holy Tradition, and a portion of Protestantism has resolved the problem in favour of human rights, ignoring the clear norm of tradition.

But back to my main theme: what we are facing today is a new post-industrial way of life, based on personal freedom from any conventions and restrictions, other than the limitations imposed by law. How should we handle this theologically? The concept of liberalism rests on the idea of liberating human beings from all that is understood as limiting their desires and their rights. Asserting the absolute value of the individual, the liberal standard takes individual freedom as the goal and means of human existence. Let me point out that this thesis is not contested by theologians, including Orthodox ones. This far we have not crossed the borderline into transgression of the teachings of the Church. For the Lord himself, creating man in His own image and likeness, placed in him the divine gift of free will. Thus, man's freedom of choice belongs to God's predetermined plan and its violation is a sin.

However, on the other side of this borderline begins the region of sly, diabolic and destructive falsehood. When the Apostle Paul calls us to freedom, he is speaking of man's destiny to be free in Christ; that is, liberated from the shackles of sin. Man finds his true freedom in being liberated from sin, from the dark powers of instinct and of evil hanging over him. The freedom of choice that man possesses has been granted to enable him to make his own independent choice of consciously submitting to the absolute and saving will of God. What is proposed to man is the path of free unification with God through complete submission to Him, becoming like Him in holiness. This is the purpose of the great gift of free will. Indeed there was nothing to stop the Creator from placing into His creation from the outset that which we desire and long for: His grace, likeness to Him, and the happy, constant sense of His presence in everything that is in us and around us. Put very prosaically, the Creator could have programmed us for super-abounding grace just as we wind up an alarm clock. But, being absolute Goodness and Freedom by nature, He deigned to communicate His property of freedom to mankind. And it is only this type of freedom that we understand as God-given.

The liberal idea does not call for any freeing from sin, because the very concept of sin is absent in liberalism. Man is allowed to behave sinfully, providing he remains within the law of the land and does not violate the freedom of another person. In other words, liberal doctrine releases man's potential for sin. A free person is entitled to reject everything that binds him and prevents him from adopting his sinful 'me'. In all this he is entirely independent of anyone but himself. In this respect, the liberal idea is diametrically opposed to Christianity, and may be justly labelled anti-Christian.

The problem we are considering is considerably complicated by the fact that modern liberalism has long outgrown the baby clothes of the philosophical emancipation of the human individual. It has continued its forward march into all spheres of human life, including economics, politics, law, religion, social relations and the organisation of society. From this liberal idea stems the generally accepted understanding of civil liberties, democratic institutions, the market economy, free competition, freedom of speech, freedom of conscience – all that is included in the concept of 'modern civilisation'.

At this juncture some people will throw up their hands in horror at the ideas I am expressing. For them, any critical examination of liberal doctrine is tantamount to the attempted assassination of the 'sacred principles' of rights and freedoms. For example, one commentator on my article 'The Conditions of Modernity', which was published in *Nezavisimaya Gazeta*, said that I advocate a society based on the precepts of Ayatollah Khomeini, and intend to light up Russia's skies with the flames of the stakes of the Inquisition.

It is important that society understands that liberal ideas are open to criticism from other political and economic thought systems – an approach which, incidentally, is totally concordant with 'liberal' principles. Such criticism is normal and healthy, just as normal as the coexistence of liberal ideas in politics, economics and social life with other models that do not share its concepts and points of view. There is therefore no reason why liberalism cannot be critiqued from a theological standpoint. It is not for the Church to define whether Russia should be monarchist, republican, capitalist, socialist or what have you. Resolving this issue is the prerogative of society as a whole and of each citizen individually. The Church can only welcome free and committed discussion on the best forms for the ordering of Russian society, on the social, economic and governmental principles on which our homeland should be based. Such discussion will also require of us a critical interpretation of certain pages of our history. On the other hand, the civil rights and freedoms, including the possibility of unconstrained existence for our Church, which have been victorious in the last decade of the development of Russia, remain in our eyes an absolute and unquestionable value.

Returning to our earlier question of how individuals, society and, ultimately, theology should respond to the challenge of the liberalisation of the modern world, we need to proceed now to examine two widely prevalent approaches to this issue, each with its particular assessment of the phenomenon, and each proposing its own model of behaviour. The first model is isolationistic. Its proponents suggest that we enter in by the 'wide gates' into a confined national and religious ghetto, shutting ourselves up against an external enemy, defending our identity and protecting it in every way possible against the alien, corrupting influences of a changing world. This view exists in some political circles and also among a certain part of our church community. But I ask you: is such isolation feasible and viable in an open, inter-permeating world which is entering into an era of scientific, economic, informational, communicational and even political integration? Yes, you can artificially insulate from the outside world a small group of people somewhere in the desert or taiga, although even the family of Old Believers that for many decades fled the world into Siberia was unable to preserve its privacy, nor indeed its very existence. But is it possible, so to speak, to send into isolation, into a sort of cloistered existence, a great church and a great country? Would not such a choice signify the rejection of the mission bequeathed by Christ the Saviour Himself to the Church, of testifying to the truth to the world?

The second option offered to us is to adopt the liberal model of civilisation in the form in which it has developed to date in the West, mechanically transfer it onto Russian soil and, if necessary, forcefully implant it into people's lives. Unlike similar attempts in the past, this no longer requires the power of the State and its institutions. That of the mass media, of advertising and the possibilities of the educational system are quite sufficient for the task. All this presupposes, of course, that our country's cultural and historical tradition is outdated, that only 'universal values' have the right to exist, and that uniformity is the sole path of integration. In this case, too, the Orthodox would find themselves in a 'spiritual reservation', the sole difference being that in the first case it would be of their own volition, in the second as punishment for refusing to surrender their religious birthright for the 'mess of pottage' of post-industrial civilisation. It is not difficult to predict that in such a situation the followers of other religious and cultural models will inevitably share the fate of the Orthodox. This second option too has its adherents both in the political world and in society at large and, to some extent, in church circles, because this new standard, under which its proponents seek to range all of God's diverse world, presents itself as a universal and comprehensive phenomenon, existing 'above barriers', as a half-way house accommodating if not all, at least a large portion of mankind.

Clearly the two models we have described above are mutually exclusive. Equally obvious is that both models enjoy quite strong support in public opinion and in political circles. The clash of these viewpoints and their numerous variants to a large extent determines the tension and confrontation we find in today's society. This tension is reflected in the life of the Church. My question therefore is: is it possible to resolve this issue peacefully, without sinning against the truth, and to propose a model of behaviour and social structure which could enable liberal and traditional ideas and values to exist side by side? Clearly this is no easy task. It calls for mutual understanding and concerted action from the parties involved. Here I can see a wide field for the co-operation of the other traditional religions, and of all the healthy forces in our society who love Russia and sincerely wish her good, with the Russian Orthodox Church, and especially with its theologians, who can help modern man to an understanding of the importance of tradition as a normative factor, as a determinant of a system of values, including the cultural, spiritual and moral orientation of the individual and society. Orthodox theology needs to lay bare the nerve-centre of the problem under discussion, insisting that the existence of liberal institutions in economics, politics, social life and inter-governmental relations is acceptable, feasible and morally justified under one condition only: the non-implantation of the principles of liberal philosophy as these pertain to the human person and interpersonal relations. But if liberal ideology is used to trigger disinhibition and the release of harmful desires, provoking an explosion of carnality and giving central place to human selfishness, if liberal institutions serve to legitimise the right to sin, then such a society, lacking norms of individual and social behaviour, is inevitably doomed to spiritual degeneration, to becoming a stage for dark and unruly passions. Under the pressure of sin unleashed and triumphant, a society accepting such a value system will sooner or later be doomed to failure. If we do not want this, then the presence of liberal ideas in political, economic and social life must be regarded by us as valid only if coupled with the clear rejection of the liberal system of values as applied to the human person.

The Church openly calls sin by its name, and devotes its efforts to saving man. One of the most important tools for achieving the goals I have just spoken about ought to be the establishing in our people of an understanding of the Orthodox faith as a norm of life. I venture to think that both those contemporary Russians who are suffering, humiliated and left to fend for themselves, and those who are relatively well situated, have a vital need for the religious way of life to be universally accepted as a natural and unconditional value. And if indeed we take liberal ideology as the model of government and society for the development of our country, then we need, in full accordance with the liberal principle of checks and balances, to counterbalance this with a policy of affirming traditional Russian values in education and interpersonal relations. The question of what form law, education, culture, social relations and public morality should take becomes the question of whether we will be able to maintain our national civilisation in the coming century, whether it will find its place in the world community of nations, and whether we survive as an Orthodox people.

I believe this will be accomplished through the prayers of all the saints who have illumined the land of Russia. May Russia's tragic experience in the twentieth century, unbearable for any other country, and not the first in our history, serve the good of all mankind, by pointing it to the danger to be avoided by all means. Under the eyes of all, Russia's resurgence in the new century can potentially provide an alternative, positive and salutary lesson to the world: that of the organising of the life of individuals and society in accordance with principles in which dependence on the moral law unites with personal and civil liberties.

How, practically, can this general approach be implemented? How can we move, not in the direction of isolationism, but towards the participation of the Church and of every Christian in the life of a modern secularised society, but subject to maintaining our Christian identity, our originality and our vision of life as defined by the Orthodox tradition?

In theory, of course, we understand that we cannot turn back the pages of history, that nostalgia for the Golden (we think) Age of Christianity 'profiteth nothing' (John 6:63), that God calls us to live here and now. But when it comes to the real business, that of developing and implementing a true, Orthodox, ecclesial relationship with the complex phenomena of modernity, we oftentimes fall prey to the sin of despondency. This is of course understandable, because the life of today's society, based on the principles of liberalism, is so arranged that religious belief is constantly 'put into brackets'.

The world seeks to oust religious motivation to the margins of social life. (As yet) no one particularly persecutes us for our own religious views ('Believe what you like, it's none of our business.'). Many times we are all too willing to accept such an arrangement, to park in the comfortable spot in the lay-by allocated to us. With our accumulated stock of spiritual values, we can sit there quite comfortably, whiling away the intervening period until the apocalyptic disaster that we see threatening a humanity speeding past us on the road towards 'progress'.

But is it right to give way to the temptation to escape from our social, cultural, political reality? We have been sent by Christ in this world for its salvation (John 17:18). The Lord ordered us not to flee from the world, not to hide from the world, but to conquer the world with our faith (1 John 5:4), to go out into the whole world, preaching the gospel (Mark 16:15) and to be the light of the world and salt of the earth (Matt. 5:13–16). Of course, this is only possible if we, remaining in the world, are people 'not of this world' (John 17:16), living not 'according to the course of this world' (Eph. 2:2), not 'after the rudiments of the world' (Col. 2:8) and distancing ourselves 'from the corruption that is in the world through lust' (2 Pet. 1–4).

The Local Council of the Russian Orthodox Church of 1917–1918 under the chairmanship of Patriarch Tikhon adopted the Decision 'On the Relationship of the Church to the State'. Not everything in this document is of equal value – in many ways it is conditioned by the circumstances of its time. But even then, on the border of the new era, the fathers of the Council rejected the presentation of faith as a 'private matter', without public significance: 'The Church of Christ ... is a new leaven, transubstantiating the entire nature of human life, and there are no elements of this life that are completely inaccessible to this leaven ... Therefore, these teachings that condemn the Christian faith to ultimate impotence in life ... relegating its purpose to the personal mood, as if a matter of taste, in fact condemn the Christian faith and act contrary to its very essence. In no sense can this "victory that overcomes the world, even our faith" be separated from life or considered as the private matter of the individual.'

The question, on the resolution of which will largely depend the future of the Church, can be formulated as follows: are we able to realise the vision of life which is born of faith, in actions that are meaningful for the community, with convincing answers to the problems of today? If not, then everything we say about the proper balance between tradition and liberalism and about the vitality of our faith and our tradition will remain only a declaration, no more than a naked structure; a lifeless, muscle-less skeleton.

The most important theological task in this regard is the development of the social teaching of the Orthodox Church, which, rooted in tradition and responding to the issues facing modern society, will serve as a guide for priests and laity, and will give the outside world a clear idea of the Church's position on the most important issues of our time.

It is clear that as long as the Church in our country was not free, the formulation of such a doctrine in anything like its full scope was impossible. The formulation of individual parts of it began soon after the Local Council in 1988, when the Church began to find itself facing hitherto unthinkable questions, such as whether bishops and priests should become involved in government and in political and public organisations. Various statements of His Holiness the Patriarch, definitions of the Holy Synod and decisions of the Archbishops' Councils of the Russian Orthodox Church of 1992, 1994 and 1997, made a significant contribution to the formulation of this social doctrine. Increasingly, however, it became clear that it was impossible for the Church to confine itself to specific responses to pressing problems. What was needed was a common doctrine that would guide the Church, not just for a year or two, but for a long period, and not only in Russia but also in the other countries of its canonical territory.

Establishing this doctrine became the task of a Synodal working group. With its remit defined by the 1994 Archbishops' Council, this group began preparing the papers for the perhaps rather clumsily named 'Concept of the Russian Orthodox Church on church–state relations and the problems of modern society as a whole'. The draft concept was to be finalised and submitted to the Archbishops' Council by the summer of 2000.

It is impossible, within the confines of a newspaper article, to give an idea of all the problems that this work needs to encompass. But let me mention here its basic themes and some of the most pressing and controversial issues.

One of the most important themes, of course, is the relationship between Church and State and the participation of the Church and its members in political life. At the 1992 Archbishops' Council it was already publicly stated that 'the Church is not bound to any public or governmental system, nor to any political force. She is above "right" or "left".' It is important, however, to set out the theological basis for such a position, rooted in the tradition of the Church, and to present a detailed comparative analysis of the origin, nature, functions and goals of the Church and of the State. Orthodox Church tradition has at times included a very special relationship to the monarchy as the preferred form of government. Today, some see such a relationship as quasi-dogmatic for the Orthodox faith, while others assert that this was entirely due to transient historical circumstances and can in no way be transplanted into the soil of modern political reality. To what extent and in what form can the historical teaching about the symphony of monarchy and the priesthood be applied to the contemporary system and structure of government?

Could it be that this ancient political ideal is founded on certain principles – of the Orthodox attitude to government as service and of the boundaries of authority of State power – that are still valid today? I want to emphasise that we are not talking here in any way about political time-serving, or about the 'fit' between our heritage and the results of any regular elections or public opinion polls. Our task lies elsewhere – it is rather to reveal how the norms of tradition can be applied to the specific circumstances of modern life.

The Hierarchy of our Church has in recent years repeatedly explained that the Plenitude of the Church is not involved in the political struggle. It does not call on people to vote for this or that party, does not identify itself with any parties, that is, partial interests. This is evident from the very catholic nature of the Church. But if we confine ourselves to saying: 'The Church stands outside of politics', will that not in fact denote the triumph of liberalism (religion as a purely personal matter, with religious organisations outside of political life)? Does the Church really have no position on political issues? Does it really have nothing to say to politicians, and do Orthodox people really have nothing to do with politics? Life insistently demands of us to indicate clearly on what basis a Christian – precisely as a Christian – can participate in the political process and in government.

The political problem intersects with the area of law in such matters as the relationship of the Church to State laws and decisions which are contrary to its understanding of the world and impede its mission (including the question of the limits of its obedience to the authorities). It is important to set out the Church's relationship to the principle of freedom of conscience (and in general to the issue of human rights). As you know, in this area too we encounter in the Church, and among theologians, mixed opinions, and it is important to understand which of these are in line with Church tradition, and which to a greater degree reflect personal views and are fed by external socio-cultural and secular philosophical ideas. The same applies to the controversial issue of the death penalty. Can we express in this case a common Church position, based not on the arguments of secular humanism, but on the norms of Holy Tradition and the experience of the Church?

Can the Church make a constructive contribution to the world-wide debate about the problems of economic, political, informational and cultural globalisation? I have already addressed this issue above. I am convinced that it is essential to formulate a Church-wide position on this issue. Such a position would provide a basis for the Church's interaction with international organisations (the UN, EU and others).

Another sensitive topic is that of Church and nation. Unfortunately, in this area, very one-sided affirmations are presented as the teaching of the Church. Some seek to deny the very concept of Christian patriotism and the right of Christians to national identity. Others effectively degrade the Orthodox faith to the role of one attribute of traditional national identity. It is therefore vital for the Church to show how, based on the word of God and Tradition, national and universal principles blend harmoniously with Christian life. These disputed questions include: can we speak of an 'Orthodox nation' and of the nation as a unique guardian of the faith? Does the Church recognise the doctrine of 'collective sin of the people' and 'general repentance' for it?

Nor can economic problems remain without proper assessment by the Church. What is the attitude of the Church towards different kinds and forms of ownership, including that of the land? Are the fruits of labour to be allocated solely on the basis of the merits of the worker or should they to some extent belong to all members of society?

Nor can the Church remain indifferent to the problems of the ecological crisis, which is becoming an increasingly critical threat to the very existence of human civilisation. For us, it is important not simply to repeat the alarmist assessments of secular experts and environmental activists, but to bring to the understanding of this challenging topic our own, more in-depth approach, rooted in the biblical understanding of the world and of man's role in it.

What answer does Orthodoxy give to the challenge of modern feminism? Should its answer be a total negation of this direction of public opinion, or can the Church, based on its historical experience, positively assess certain aspects of the idea of political, social and cultural equality for women? What position does the Church take towards the discourse on the position of sexual minorities and on the future of the family which predicts an evolution towards 'multiple forms of cohabitation'? What can be the religious and moral assessment of 'family planning'?

Particularly difficult are the problems of bioethics, with the new biomedical technologies at times presenting us with ethical and legal issues inconceivable at the time of the Ecumenical Councils. What is the status of the human embryo, when does it become a human being? Only when you can recognise that a person has already died? Can I use his organs for transplants? Are the pre-natal diagnosis of disease or 'genetic certification' of all births good or bad? Why cannot people be cloned? How do we evaluate reproductive technologies to overcome infertility from the Orthodox point of view?

The easiest way is to say 'As late as yesterday we knew nothing of this – all this is from the evil one', and remain in our isolated circle, fencing ourselves off from this vain world. It is much harder, but much more fruitful, to try to develop a theological, thoughtful assessment, and, if we say 'No, you can't', to explain why, and, if we say 'Yes, you can', to indicate why we are in agreement. Such work of course requires the co-operation of physicians, geneticists and philosophers. We must also take into account here the experience of our Orthodox brethren in the West who have already encountered similar problems.

It may also be useful to study the positions of other faiths. Our aim should be not the arithmetic mean between extremes, not a set of arguments borrowed from all sides – 'here a little and there a little' (Isa. 28:10) – but precisely the Orthodox, religiously-grounded approach, the development of which is the creative task of modern Orthodox theology.

The same can be said about the work on the social doctrine of the Church in general. In conclusion, I would like to express the purpose of this work in the words of a remarkable St Petersburg priest and professor of theology, my father's teacher, Mikhail Cheltsov, whom the Bolsheviks twice sentenced to death and eventually executed. As early as ten years before the October Revolution, he wrote of how he saw the task of the Church in a changing society, where its influence could no longer be supported through the State structures. Above all, he pointed out that Christianity should be 'manifested in life in all its inherent strength, revealed in the unity of being of faith and life and producing a Christian way of government, way of being society, economy, culture, science – in short, to Christianise life in all its manifestations'.

And the last thing I want to say, thinking about the task of theology in relation to the Church and the world, is that a faith-based norm of life, as captured in the Apostolic Tradition and guarded in the Church, will manifest to us its fullness and its real worth once Christians themselves are filled with the desire to put into practice what they have learned. And to this task are called not just theologians, but the entire Fullness of the Church, under the leading of the Holy Spirit.

Chapter 2

A COMMON APPROACH TO CHURCH UNITY AND THE RENEWAL OF MANKIND

Paper given to an international seminar in Budapest,
14–18 December 1987

The theme I have been invited to speak on – a common approach to Church unity and the renewal of mankind – immediately confronts us with a methodological problem: Church unity relates uniquely to the activities of Christians, while the renewal of mankind concerns every man and woman on our planet. How can we talk of a common approach to these two problems? We may discover one or the other general principle, but otherwise our approaches will be as different as are the two problems. At the same time, Church unity and the renewal of mankind are deeply inter-related. In other words, the title of my paper covers at least three themes: church unity, the renewal of mankind, and their inter-relationship, each of which calls for separate treatment. To keep within my appointed time frame, I want to focus on one of these themes and examine the bases for this common search for the renewal of mankind and look at the specific contribution Christians can make to it.

What do we mean by the 'renewal of mankind'? Implicit in this wording is the idea that the human condition is unsatisfactory and that action is needed to change it for the better. Also, the fact that we are talking about humanity as a whole and not individual nations and states, tells us that the problems that cloud our lives are global in nature, and that solving them will call for concerted action across the planet. However, the ability to make take joint action presupposes a certain unity. Which begs the fundamental question: in what sense can one speak of unity in relation to mankind as a whole? What does such unity imply?

We can approach this concept on several levels. In the Acts of the Apostles, St Paul says: 'From one blood He (God) has made the whole human race' (Acts 17:26). From this affirmation comes the well-known theological concept of the unity of the human race, constituting a single family bound by invisible mystical ties. Evidence of this mystical unity is provided by the irresistible desire of people to enter into different forms of association. One of the axioms of our lives is that the human person can realise himself only through communication with other individuals. In isolation from his fellows, man cannot achieve fullness of life; he is doomed to destruction. All human activities, conscious and unconscious, associate us in one way or another with our fellow-men.

This mystical unity I have just mentioned is embodied in different social structures. The reasons for this unifying activity in our sin-damaged world can often be very prosaic, and this activity can also take on ugly and at times dangerous forms. But even this does not prevent it from being an expression of a universal human desire for unity, based on a sense of common ontological roots. Throughout history human communities have tried, with greater or lesser success (and at times have blatantly failed), to implement the idea of human unity. While at the level of family, clan, clan, tribe, nation and state, these attempts have produced certain results, at the higher, inter-state level, they have almost always ended in failure. The most obvious historical example is aggressive wars and the empires emerging from them. As well as satisfying the ambitions, greed, power-lust and vanity of conquerors, and aside from the military-strategic, political and economic objectives, empire-building in a certain way expresses a subconscious desire for unity, for a blurring of national and other boundaries. Within the vast world of an empire, a single state body is created as the essential precondition for social communality. History tells us, however, that such experiments, based primarily on force, are inevitably doomed. Counteracting this unifying force are the centrifugal tendencies generated by frustration at the uneven distribution of wealth and at the swallowing up of the cultures of the peoples brought into this union. In the very nature of things, a community of people achieved by force and maintained by a balance of power can never be strong and durable. But even on a voluntary basis and in the absence of any coercion, the unity of mankind can hardly be expressed and accommodated within a single state, at least in the foreseeable future.

What then do we have in mind in calling for the unity of mankind? How can we describe this unity in categories that are clear and convincing not just for Christians but for all our contemporaries? How can we proclaim the biblical message of the unity of the human race, without ignoring the cruel realities of the modern world? These realities require us to use more reserved language, at least towards the non-Christian world. The idea of 'unity of mankind', almost incomprehensible in itself, needs to be made explicit in concrete, realistic concepts if this Christian message is to have any chance of being heard in our divided and contradictory world. And even these concepts may only be partially able to convey the biblical message of the oneness of humanity. Maybe they will be not solid food, but milk, for feeding not 'spiritual', but 'carnal' and mutually-separated people (1 Cor. 3:1–2).

Our starting point in defining such concepts has to be the threat that hangs over all mankind. This is a global threat: in today's world there is no magic oasis where people can feel safe and secure. We live in a confined and interdependent world, and the only way in which we can resolve the global crises is for all of us, the whole of humanity, to do so together.

It is a well-known fact that an external threat has the effect of increasing the internal unity and cohesiveness of any state. A general danger forces people to put aside their internal differences. Without this unity, there is little chance of defeating the enemy. Today, the whole of mankind has common mortal enemies. The whole of human civilisation finds itself under siege, faced with the eternal question of 'to be or not to be?', posed, for first time ever, on a planetary scale. Faced with these threats humanity has no other path but to unite. In other words, the unity of mankind that is effectively achievable is a unity of action in the fight for universal human survival. It is important to state clearly at this juncture that such unity is a pragmatic one, falling far short of Christian aspirations. It is, rather, the first step on the long journey. At the same time it is also clear that without this first step there may not be any path to journey along at all.

The main difficulty in uniting humanity to overcome the crises threatening it lies in the very nature of these crises, not external to mankind, but generated by mankind itself. They are its internal diseases.

In the past, such diseases were treated on the familiar pattern: one state or one part of the world sought to solve its problems on the back of another state or another part of the world. Such 'therapy' was always carried out from a position of strength. The winner was the one who was stronger. This was the very basis of global politics. The driving force behind this policy was national self-interest, cloaked in the mantle of national security. The realities of today's interdependent world reveal the utter bankruptcy of this policy. Any attempt to improve one's own position at the expense of someone else's turns into a phantom gain, exacerbating the crisis and harming not only the weaker, but also the stronger side. Global economic processes provide convincing illustration of this. In the military domain too, sticking with the old patterns will logically lead to universal destruction. In other words, humanity must learn to overcome the threats facing it by working together, following a new principle that the preservation of the interests of each is the precondition for the achievement of the interests of all, just as the security of each is the precondition for the security of all.

However, the proclamation of this principle immediately leads to the question of criteria. What do we mean when we say the interests and security of everyone? States and peoples can have very differing understandings of these concepts. To represent the complexity of the problem it is enough to take, for example, a category like material well-being, the understanding of which is always an individual matter. In other words, joint actions to address the issues facing humanity need to be based on a common world view. Without such a basis it is impossible to achieve any general coherent understanding of these issues, let alone overcome them. Without such a basis there can be no unity of humanity to confront contemporary crises.

Does this mean that we must reject any idea of a common ideological basis as pure utopia? The extraordinary variety and often contradictory nature of existing worldviews do indeed make the implementation of this idea very much more complicated. And yet in our day there are encouraging signs, suggesting that the ice has started to break, that, faced with risks that threaten the whole of humanity, people are beginning to understand the need to find common principles. Principles that rise above ideological, religious, national and class interests and that could provide a true basis of unity and co-ordinated action in today's crises.

To understand in which categories this framework can be defined, we need to try and find a common factor in the various contemporary crises. Unfortunately, these crises are too numerous to list here. They are developing against a background of unprecedented scientific and technological progress – that same progress in which the romantics of the past saw a panacea for all ills, and through which they placed great hope in the future. 'Technological euphoria' was all too common in the 1960s in the search both for Church unity and the renewal of humanity.[1] But by the 1970s the mood had already become more realistic. The energy crisis of 1973 with all its economic and political consequences exposed the extreme vulnerability of our contemporary scientific and technological civilisation and its dependence on resources that no longer appeared inexhaustible.

However, the 1970s brought something more important in the assessment of scientific and technological progress. Even those who had been carried away by the earlier euphoria began to talk about 'changing course', of the need to 'consciously clarify the rules of our community' and 'reach agreement on the principles by which we wish to live with each other'.[2] Discussion about the dangerous consequences of scientific and technological progress included deep reflection on the moral condition of modern man and society.[3] Indeed, the threat of self-destruction hanging over humanity began to be seen as a result of the triumph of its scientific thought – its power over the forces of nature. On the way people manage this power, it was realised, depends the future of life itself. The fact that the tremendous advances in science and technology have got us no further towards resolving global crises tells us that we are not making good use of our power. Indeed, scientific and technological development serves to escalate crises, fuelled by material force (the arms race, ecology) and, in certain parts of the world, by economic oppression (transnational corporations).

Why? What is the mysterious rationale that converts scientific and technical progress into the flywheel of world crises? Let me quote here the Russian religious thinker N. A. Berdyaev, who already back in 1932 said that 'when such terrible force lies in man's hands, the fate of mankind depends on man's spiritual condition'[4]. Science and technology today offer people an opportunity to do good or evil on a truly cosmic scale, engaging the very forces of nature in their activities. But good and evil are moral categories. They belong to man's inner world, a world that is revealed outwardly by actions of every kind. Are not the disasters that we see around us the outer expression of mankind's internal diseases? Do not the crisis-like consequences of scientific and technological progress point to a lack of spiritual progress, do they not witness to the ever-widening gap between the intellectual and moral state of the world? Somehow one divines an inter-dependence between the development of modern civilisation and spiritual decline of the individual. Scientific and technological progress offers modern man a more comfortable life-style and an easier means of livelihood. At the same time, a lack of stable moral norms pushes people, with their increased power, to seek ever greater comfort and wealth. This upward spiralling of material power is accompanied by discouraging developments in the field of ethical values, with morality seen as an unnecessary obstacle in the search for happiness, irrelevant to the pursuit of wealth and power.

In turn, the neglect of moral values further increases the importance of material values, stimulating the accumulation of personal possessions. However, it is a commonly observed fact that when people become careless with moral values, individuals begin to focus exclusively on their own well-being and ignore the interests of other people, until we arrive at a complete disdain for human life. This is what is happening in the world today. This is the spiritual and moral essence of the multiple crises we constantly face. We can say that today's crises demonstrate a violation of the harmony of being that is achieved through the implementation in human life of absolute moral values. Therefore, without minimising the role of well-known political, economic, historical and other factors in determining the face of contemporary crises, we can rightly state that their root causes lie in the human spirit, in human morality. And if so, then humanity must take up the fight against these crises on the basis of shared moral principles. In other words, the ideological basis needed to bring about a unification of the human spirit in the struggle for survival can be described in moral categories that are common to all.

Such an ideological basis seems, also, to be the only really feasible solution today. And the reason for this lies not only in the variety, contradictions and even mutual hostility of the world's ideologies, but rather in the unique, universal and absolute nature of human morality. Even if, arguing from the multiplicity of the ethical codes of people living in different social, cultural and economic conditions, many thinkers cast doubt on the moral consciousness of humanity, the possibility of arriving at generally accepted ethical objectives governing the behaviour of all human being, with a unified system of values, is widely accepted. The different codes that exist in different parts of the world are to be regarded rather as differing parts of the one whole.[5]

One result of a purely rationalistic, pragmatic attitude to the organisation of human society has been to reduce attention to the importance of morality in public life. The mistake of politicians, scientists and lawyers has been effectively to separate politics, science and law from ethics. Of course, this separation has never been explicitly proclaimed by anyone, and in theory the moral principle is generally recognised as superior to the principle of law. However, in practice the moral order falls more into the field of 'good intentions', useful advice and exhortations. With its emphasis over many centuries on the personal dimension of ethics, the Christian Church has in a sense helped create an atmosphere which has caused an 'ethical secularisation' of public life. This 'ethical secularisation' has cost humanity dearly. Millions of victims, especially in the wars of the twentieth century, bespeak the neglect, in political life, of the undiminished importance of absolute moral values, or else the attempt to interpret morality in the direction of national, class or racial interests.

The bitter experience of both past and contemporary crises convinces us that social and economic relations, politics and science cannot stand outside the realm of ethics. The only way to improve the world we live in is by observing and protecting the eternal and immutable moral principles of life.

However, the level of application of moral standards in public life is dependent on the moral level of the people. Without the ability to distinguish between good and evil, without a sense of duty and responsibility, without self-control and self-limitation, the human personality is incapable of healthy social life. From personal morality derives what has been called 'natural law'. This natural law asserts that fair and reasonable order which, according to the Russian philosopher, S. L. Frank, in concrete conditions most closely corresponds to the moral nature of man. The criterion of reasonableness of such an order is provided by a society that acts to ensure the implementation of the higher moral principles of human existence. The idea of 'natural law' derives from the principle of unity, integrity and indivisibility of human morality. It assumes an indissoluble link between the personal and the general. The spheres of personal morality and of social morality are interrelated and interdependent. Frank puts it as follows: 'These two areas have an inner inter-connection. This connection is formed by the layer of human life, which we can call the area of customs, habits, everyday moral teaching ... Via this intermediate sphere the overall legal order or legislation, which sets the rules for the overall system of collective human life, is ultimately the expression and product of the personal spiritual lives of the members of society, and of their degree of moral perfection or imperfection.'[6] 'The quality of any social structure is a function of the moral level of the people of which it is constituted.'[7] From this Frank concludes, in line with the ethical concepts of classical Russian literature and of Gogol and Dostoevsky in particular, that 'the path to the most effective and lasting results is the one that leads from the inside outwards, from personal life to public life'[8]. The moral integrity of society is the sum of the moral integrities of individual human beings. And on this inter-relatedness depends the very survival of the human race (a relationship that AIDS has made clear for even the most inexperienced). Evil has its own dynamic, the logical conclusion of which is death and oblivion. If evil is not opposed at every level of existence, its multiplication will ultimately destroy the world. Evil brings chaos and formlessness, a 'Dionysian principle', entropy. This entropy allows evil to grow to its logical end, which is death. The preservation of life therefore calls for spiritual effort. A man who has lost his moral foundations, his spiritual connectedness to the world of other people, and to nature, is a danger to the planet. With today's technical and scientific potential, evil ceases to be a private matter, even for those of us who do not have our fingers on the atomic trigger and do not control nuclear reactors.

A surprising discovery of our time is what some would call this relationship between morality and survival. In fact it is not that novel at all. More than a hundred years ago, confessing his Christian moral principles, Dostoyevsky said: 'Beauty will save the world'. Our day and age only illustrate this interdependence. Indeed, there is only one force that can stop the growth of evil, and halt the entropy of the world. This force is the good being done by every human being singly and all together. Never before have people had such a strong motivation – that of sheer physical survival – to shun evil and do good. If you want to live, do good; live in accordance with the moral norms inscribed by God in human nature and identifiable in the norms of universal morality. There is no other way to survive. 'What is peace?', asks St Gregory of Nyssa. 'Nothing other than the implementation of love', he replies.[9] The moral principle needs to become the categorical imperative in personal and public life, providing the necessary guidance in building international relations and achieving scientific and technological progress. Moral values should be given top priority in undertaking the tasks arising in the path of human history.

Returning to the theme of the unity of humanity in the face of the crises that threaten it, and recognising that moral norms are both the way to overcome these crises and the basis for such unity, we would once again stress that this conclusion is conditioned by the very nature of man as moral being. Another famous Russian philosopher, Vladimir Solovyov, argued that, despite all the diversity and uniqueness of each human person, 'there are irreducible foundations of human morality, on which any significant construction has to be built'[10]. This moral basis is something different from the multitude of moral codes that exist today. The search for common ethical standards, expressing the very essence of the moral nature of man, needs to be the subject of dialogue between religions and ideologies. In other words, the current multiplicity of moral codes needs to make way today for a single moral code, based on absolute moral norms. Consensus on a jointly-accepted system of values arrived at through such wide-ranging dialogue would free humanity from the incompleteness and one-sidedness of each separate code.

Such a system would need to establish the interrelationship and interdependence of values and have clearly expressed priorities. The central tenet, or backbone, of such a common moral code must be the unity and indissolubility of absolute moral standards, and also the organic interrelationship and interdependence of personal and public moral ideals. Without this inner integrity, such a code will be a fiction and can never become a factor in a genuine renewal of mankind.

The most important consequence of the application of a common moral code in the field of international relations would be the possibility of developing uniform criteria for evaluating concepts like national interests and national security. This, in turn, could facilitate the realisation of the only acceptable principle for international politics in the nuclear age: the maintenance of the interests of each is the precondition for achieving the interests of all, the security of each is the precondition for the security of all. Security built on the principles of moral order would eliminate fear and suspicion, selfishness and mistrust. Recognition of the interdependence of nations and peoples would be the best stimulus for the development of trust. The integration of moral standards into public life would help solve the problems of political, economic and social justice, achieve genuine respect for human rights, and overcome the barriers between East and West, North and South.

It is important that any common moral code arrived at through broad dialogue between religions and ideologies not be a syncretic mishmash of ethical concepts, to the detriment of truth. A common moral code cannot be a compromise between ethical concepts, but must be the jointly-formulated basis of universal morality, rooted in the moral nature of man. For the same reason such a code cannot conflict with the core values of Gospel ethics, which map out the natural moral law invested by God in human nature.

A common moral code would give Christians, together with the representatives of other world religions, an opportunity to express their commitment to eternal moral truths.

Needless to say, the universal adoption of a unified body of moral norms should not entail negative consequences such as universal standardisation and unification. A common moral code can not claim the role of mandatory universal law, repealing existing legislation, but should represent a moral basis on which to align the entire corpus of national laws and international agreements. In other words, the moral code is intended to humanise the realm of politics and law, while preserving a pluralism of social and political beliefs, economic systems, culture, traditions and national customs.

However, we need to recognise that the embodiment of the idea of a general moral code will run into difficulties in two ways. First, there are the theoretical difficulties associated with the formation of the corpus of such a code of universally-recognised norms of morality; and second, the practical difficulties of implementing these standards in the modern world. These theoretical difficulties relate not only to the fundamental question of the existence and nature of (absolute or relative) norms of human morality, but also to reaching agreement on a moral assessment of the challenges facing modern man.

It is no secret that in the past the immutable body of Christian ethics has never been fully implemented in the life of Christian peoples, nor in their relationships one with another. Of course one can argue that Christianity inherited the difficult legacy of the pagan world, built on slavery and despotism. It is also true that Christianity's influence is seen in the mitigation of the cruelty of slave states and their gradual humanisation. But the fact remains that the full implementation of the system of Christian ethics was never achieved, either in Byzantium, or in medieval Europe. In Europe, the existence of a single Christian moral code did not prevent wars, including religious ones. Even if we can cast doubt on just how perfect Christian life was in the Middle Ages, even if we can say that the peoples of the earth were only partially Christianised, we cannot but recognise the fact of the failure of this historic attempt. The example of history is not absolute proof, but rather an analogy, but it can raise serious doubts as to whether human unity has ever been achieved on the basis of moral consensus.

And in this regard one can pose another dramatic question. Are today's current crises exclusively crises of an extra-Christian secularised world, or do they relate to the inner life of Christianity? It is clear that the failure of godless morality, its inability to keep people from moral degradation, with all the ensuing consequences, stands clear today for all today to see. But we should not pretend that all is well in Christianity, nor should we maintain that what is happening in today's society is not connected with the situation inside the Christian world. It is clear that the responsibility for the state of the world falls also on Christians. The problems of the modern world are connected not only with the impoverishment of faith, but also with internal diseases of Christianity, related not to its mystical and grace-given nature, but to its human nature. It is therefore important that Christians understand and grasp the meaning of what is happening in the world, and, in Christianity itself, that they comprehend the significance of world crises and correlate these crises with their internal state. Is it not this internal state that provides the first explanation of Christianity's failure to implement its ethical principles throughout history? And the reason for this lies not in Christian ethics itself, but in the quality of Christian life. H. Küng is right when he says that 'if the world changes too little, then the blame lies not with the fundamental programme of Christianity, nor with Christ Himself, but with Christians!'[11]

The moral and spiritual renewal of humanity needs to begin in the Christian environment with the commitment by Christians themselves to the complete and indissoluble norms of evangelical morality, and with the organic combination of the personal and social dimensions of Christian ethics in daily life. Any priority given to the one or the other entails the division of what are in essence undivided moral norms, distorting the structure of Christian life and weakening the Christian witness.

But is not all this wishful thinking? If in the past you were unable to unite nations and peoples on the basis of the common moral code of Christianity, why should one now take seriously the idea of unity of mankind through a common moral code? If for decades, for all the great enthusiasm, the search for Christian unity has not achieved its goal, where do these continuing hopes for the future come from? There is one simple answer to this question. This is that never before has the question of the unity of mankind been directly linked to the issue of the survival of human civilisation. After all, last but not least, it is precisely the division of the human race, including the division of Christianity, with all its consequences, that has brought our civilisation to a fatal stage. Humanity stands on the threshold of the third millennium, but it remains unclear how it will step over it. Could it be that the perception of the dangers ahead will help mankind achieve what has escaped it throughout its entire history?

There would, however, appear to be one vital precondition for achieving the unity of the Church and the renewal of humanity. This condition is repentance. Repentance – *metanoia* – is the turning away from the old order and mindset, and the awareness of and rejection of falsehood; it is restructuring (*perestroika*) in the deepest sense of the word.

It is no accident that the film *Repentance* by Georgian director T. Abuladze was the main event in the cultural life of our society at the very beginning of the *perestroika* process. Recalling the tragic events of the recent past, this film helped many of us to a deep awareness that without the rejection – however bitter – of falsehood, there can be no change for the better, either now or in the future. But repentance is both rejection and affirmation. Repentance is a genuine renewal, the implementation of truth, the restoration of beauty and truth, calling for not only humility, but also courage and daring. Repentance is a spiritual deed, committed in the name of the renewal of life.

Can the renewal of the world be achieved without spiritual struggle, without heroism, without recourse to eternal moral values?

'Say, does this street lead to the church?' the elderly woman asks the film's heroine. 'No, this street does not lead to the church', the latter replies knowingly, because of the tragic childhood memories this street carries for her, and because the church – the symbol of eternal moral values – has long been blown up. The last words of the film are the words of the astonished old lady: 'Why is this a street if it does not lead to a church?'

1 Steinbuch, K., *Falsch programmiert*, Stuttgart, 1968.
2 Steinbuch, K., *Kurskorrektur*, Stuttgart, 1973.
3 Of particular interest here is the WCC conference 'Faith, Science and the Future', held in Boston in 1979.
4 Berdyaev, N. A., *Duchovnoe sostoyanie sovremennogo mira* (Spiritual state of the current world) // (Put' – 1932, no. 35, p. 59).
5 cf. Lossky, N., *Uslovya absolytnogo dobra* (Conditions of absolute good (Paris, 1949)). Drawing on ethnographic research, we are convinced that 'all the basic moral ideas contained in the Ten Commandments are the common heritage of all mankind ...', and the moral codes of the different people give 'sufficient material for an inductive substantiation of the truth of unity of the moral conscience of humanity' (ibid., p. 130). The surprising consensus among all religions on moral responsibility and moral values only confirms this conclusion, which is not only inductive but also finds an intuitive basis in people's personal experiences.
6 Frank, S. L., *Svet vo t'me* (Light in the darkness), Paris, 1949, pp. 378–379.
7 idem p. 381.
8 idem p. 379.
9 Svyatitel Grigoriy Nisskij (St Gregory of Nyssa), *Tvorenija* (Works) Part 2, Moscow, 1861, p. 458.
10 Soloviev, V., *Pervichnye dannye nravstvennosti*/Voprosy filosofii i psikhologii (The primary data of morality/Philosophical and Psychological questions), p. 361.
11 Küng, H., *On Being a Christian*, Munich, 1974.

Chapter 3

LIBERAL IDEOLOGY: A THREAT TO PEACE AND FREEDOM

Published in Tserkovny Vestnik, *no. 1–2 (278–279), January 2004*

With two world wars now fading into history, the peoples of Western Europe can look back on almost 60 years of peace. However, we Christians should not forget St Paul's words that: 'when they shall say: "Peace and safety", then sudden destruction shall come upon them … Therefore let us not sleep as others do, but watch and be sober' (1 Thess. 5:3, 6).

At the beginning of the third millennium, following the collapse of communism, mankind faces the threat of new conflicts, rooted in issues of power and values. Two antagonistic systems are ranged against each other in today's world, one secular and humanistic, the other religious and traditionalist. On the one hand is the liberal view of the individual and of society, and on the other an approach founded in traditional cultures and religions. By liberal we are referring to the secular, humanistic approach to the organisation of society and the State, derived from Western philosophy and political thought, as perceived, learned and developed in Western Europe and North America. It is this view which, in the twentieth century, formed the basis for the activities of international organisations. Currently, the liberal 'standard' presents itself as a universal norm for structuring social life, and government at the planetary level. The legal and political framework shaped by this standard is proclaimed as the norm, departures from which are severely censured or punished by force.

This is a cause of great discomfort to the huge masses of people who live outside of Western Europe and North America and who continue to be guided in their daily lives by other values – especially those deriving from their religious and cultural traditions. At the intellectual level, the clash of these views also produces enormous tension. Many times the representatives of liberalism refuse to admit the possibility of their values being open to review. They ignore the very principle of liberalism – the licitness and admissibility of disagreement – just as soon as any challenge is uttered to their universalist pretensions. On the other hand, many representatives of traditional values reject out of hand any thought of reaching a consensus with their opponents, whose views they brand as sinful and alien to the religious understanding of the world and man. This situation is reinforced by the history of liberal ideas, which emerged in the West outside any real influence of Islam, Judaism, Buddhism, Hinduism and Orthodoxy. The role of Catholic theology in this process is also far from clear. Much more certain is the involvement in this process of Protestantism, itself an attempt at a liberal reading of the Christian message.

Today, unfortunately, very few people are talking about the need for serious and open-minded dialogue between liberal, secular humanist, religious and cultural traditions. At conferences exploring this area, discussion focuses exclusively on inter-faith relations. The liberal-humanist component is almost always absent as a player in this field, even if, in evaluating a particular religious concept, a secular liberal-humanist cliché is all too often imposed and the concept is evaluated positively or negatively based on its concordance with the Western liberal standard. Vivid examples of such evaluation, incidentally, are the criticisms voiced in the West to the 'basic social concept of the Russian Orthodox Church'.

Today's world needs both real inter-religious dialogue, especially between Christians and Muslims, and dialogue between religious and secular-humanistic thought. The aim of such dialogue should be to build a multi-polar world. And by poles we should understand here not so much the poles of political power (though they too come into the picture), but cultural and civilisational poles. Neither globalisation, nor indeed, European integration, can be founded on a mono-civilisational basis. The very idea is a dangerous delusion, reminiscent of the 'sole correct and scientifically based' teaching of Marx, Engels and Lenin. The idea of a single philosophical concept, imposable on the whole world and embracing the diversity of cultural and religious traditions, is simply a non-starter. From the perspective of most religious traditions it is very difficult, if not impossible, to accept the primacy of the values proclaimed by the modern liberal 'standard': the priority of the earthly life over eternal life, and of personal freedom and rights over the moral demands of faith and the values of a religious way of life. Large numbers of people are frustrated by the practical effects of liberal standards in economics and politics: the rich get richer and richer, and the poor get poorer and poorer. 'Managed globalisation' of the world economy is generating and perpetuating poverty and powerlessness among the peoples of the 'second' and 'third' worlds. Despite this, the proponents of liberalism continue to argue that their policy has no alternative. Is this true? No economic model of development should be called successful if it fails to solve social problems, if it does not give people the opportunity to control their destiny. Economic imbalances in the world not only maintain, but are constantly reinforcing the capacity for hatred, creating instability and fuelling terrorism. The liberal political elites who promised and continue to promise freedom to the world are quick to apply very stringent measures to 'educate' and 'instruct' those human communities that insist on other social orders.

A second, smaller-scale and less discussed, but no less significant example is education: in the public schools of many countries, including Russia, materialist ideology and secular humanism are a mandatory part of the curriculum. Religious values are replaced, or, where tolerated, are subjected to major restrictions that often deprive children of any real right of choice. This religious worldview is artificially contrasted with the so-called scientific worldview, supposedly the only one of real benefit to society.

Exemplary in this connection is the silence on Christian values in discussion of the draft constitution for the European Union. Christians should not, however, be afraid to declare publicly that without moral values, freedom, democracy, human rights and the dignity of the individual are meaningless and can turn into the opposite! This we know from historical experience. Europe remains a spiritual and cultural force in the modern world, not only because over the past two centuries she has learned secular humanism, but also and largely because a centuries-old Christian tradition is still alive there. Western Christianity continues to exist not because it has adapted itself to an outside ideology. Its strength lies rather in its historical heritage and in its being the living faith of millions of ordinary people. The fact that the collapse of the Soviet Union did not turn into a bloody mess was not because 'enlightened' people in Moscow, Kiev and Washington modelled the peace process. No, simply because our people – Orthodox, Muslim or of other religions – had, even after decades of state atheism, maintained a sense of conscience and morality.

All of which begs the question: if the European Union is to become a common home for many nations, should the secular-humanistic model of society and the state enjoy a monopoly right in it? Should we not rather give serious consideration to the possibility of religious and moral influence on the social order?

Talking about religious values, of course, I mean not just Christian values. At this stage our opponents craftily argue that Christian values cannot be mentioned in the EU constitution, because Europe is also home to Muslims, Jews, Buddhists, Hindus and other non-Christians. But the latter are in fact the last to advocate the deletion of references to Christian values in the preamble to the European constitution, because the moral values that are fundamental to Christianity are largely shared by the other traditional religions.

It is important that the legislators of the new Europe listen to the position of believers, for whom secular-liberal values alone are inadequate, as indeed they are inadequate for society as a whole. Eliminating as they do the concepts of sin and personal responsibility, these values and freedoms are unable to halt the moral degradation of society, because they objectively promote the freedom of fallen man, freedom outside any moral system. This freedom turns into tyranny, into the violence of sublimated passions and the destruction of moral bearings in personal, family and social life.

To function well, the new Europe needs to understand that human rights, peace and harmony can be truly realised only through a sense of duty and responsibility, and only within a concrete system of moral values.

In our day, faith is a key factor in determining the way of life and behaviour of millions of people. The many Christians and believers of other religions who hold that faith is more important than worldly prosperity, that solidarity is no less important than individual self-fulfilment, that traditional values are no less important than economic success, justice no less than material prosperity, and that the welfare of one's home country stands above personal gain, are also entitled to have their beliefs reflected in the existing social order. Otherwise conflict becomes inevitable.

What is more, a traditional consciousness, critical of the dominance of the liberal 'standard', can under certain conditions become a breeding ground for extremism, including religious extremism. The threat of terrorism arises whenever and wherever political radicals are able to convince people to take up arms to defend their values. With secular Western values today shared by the most powerful nations and forced by them onto other peoples, terrorism, to which these nations remain vulnerable, is seen by the opposing party as the only effective way to fight back. The world situation is aggravated by the fact that fanatical religious radicals do not just appeal to religious and traditional values, do not just protect the lifestyles of their own peoples, but seek the global spread and domination of their religious and political views and beliefs. Terrorism in the twenty-first century is not an inter-religious conflict; it is not a war between Christians and Muslims, it is a conflict between the new world order based on secular liberal values, and those who, exploiting religious and traditional values, seek to impose their own world order. Such conflict is potentially endless. Neither military nor police measures can save people from the threat of terrorism. Events in today's world are clear evidence of this.

And yet, humanity must say a categorical 'no' to any political exploitation of religious beliefs by radicals, fanatics, and just plain bandits. We must strongly condemn terrorism in all its forms and manifestations and recognise the right of states to protect their citizens, by force if necessary. In so doing we must also, however, avoid double standards: if you denounce the evildoers who killed innocent people in Manhattan, you must equally condemn terrorist acts in Chechnya, Moscow, Kosovo and elsewhere on our planet.

Ensuring the truly sustainable existence of the human community calls for a new world order, multi-polar and multi-structured. Religious and other traditional models will also need to be taken into account in formulating a common civilisational pattern. It is time to give back to society an understanding of religion as the deepest layer of human culture, not confinable to personal or family life.

Let me state once yet again: what we need today is not only inter-religious dialogue, but also dialogue between believers and the upholders of a secular worldview. The latter need to understand that their outlook is not entirely 'neutral' and 'objective' and cannot serve as the unique, non-alternative basis for social order. A world based only on a single ideological model will be unsustainable. It will be powerless to prevent new and bloody wars in the twenty-first century.

To avoid such developments, we must take national and religious traditions into account whenever we apply international standards at local, national level. To prevent future wars, it is important to create conditions in which each nation can develop freely within its own religious and cultural traditions.

To criticise the monopoly in Europe and the world of a single civilisational model is not to reject out of hand the values inherent in this model, nor the possibility of harmonising these values with the moral ideas of traditional religions. Indeed it is vitally important, through dialogue between secular and religious worldviews, to ensure such harmonisation. For me, the starting point for such harmonisation lies both in the rights and freedoms of the individual and in the moral values that are expressed through religious traditions.

In conclusion, let me state once again that the crisis of globalisation facing mankind can be overcome only by the combined efforts of all believers and all people of goodwill in the moral education of the individual, and in shaping just and viable foundations for human coexistence.

Chapter 4

GOD'S PLAN FOR MAN
AND FREE WILL

Address to the International Theological Conference, 'Eschatological Teaching of the Church', Moscow, 14 November 2005

Discussion of contemporary socio–political issues largely devolves around the concept of freedom. In order to join in this debate in a meaningful fashion, it important for us to understand this concept, which is fundamental to human existence, in the light of the Orthodox tradition. On this basis we will then able to evaluate the various interpretations of freedom in modern political thought and in derivative ideologies.

In my view, a clear and concise Christian approach to the problem of freedom is expressed by Fyodor Dostoevsky, who states, in *The Brothers Karamazov*, that 'the devil wrestles with God, but his battle-field is people's hearts'. This sentence from the pen of the great Russian writer expresses, as we shall see, the very essence of the traditional Eastern Christian perspective on this issue, as well as placing the question of human will into an eschatological perspective. Indeed, in this confrontation between good and evil, man's right of self-determination becomes a decisive factor in the destiny of creation.

Indeed, the Orthodox patristic tradition talks not so much about freedom as such, but about human will. Following this custom, we will first consider the concept of will, in order to be then able to draw conclusions about the concept of freedom. The true meaning of the concept of will was disclosed at the Incarnation.

It was the Word made flesh that revealed what man is intended to be in his perfect state, what his will should be, and what his freedom consists of. It is therefore not surprising that the Orthodox under-standing of human will was formulated in the context of the theo-logical disputes concerning the will of Christ, which took place in the seventh century and resulted in condemnation by the Sixth Ecumenical Council of the false teaching on the absence of human will in Christ.

What, then, is the human will in terms of the Incarnation? Will is an integral and immanent part of human nature. Without it, man can not be considered a rational creature. In both the ancient philosophi-cal tradition and in classical Christian theology, this notion has been inseparably linked with the category of the intellect, what the ancients called *nous*, the most important part of the human being, which, according to the ancient philosophers and the Fathers of the Church, distinguishes man from the rest of the universe, placing him on the highest level of the visible world.

It is the human will that is involved in the most terrible tragedy in history – the Fall. Wishing to taste the forbidden fruit from the tree of knowledge of good and evil, man allowed sin to enter his nature. Sin in the first place affected the human will, through which decay and death entered the human race. That is why the human will, which the Word took upon himself by becoming flesh, is vital to salvation from sin. This idea we find in St Maximus the Confessor: 'If Adam partook willingly, then the will is the first part of us to have been subjected to passion. If, as they (the Monothelites) say, the Word, on becoming incarnate, did not take on human will with human nature, then I am not freed from sin. And if I have not been freed from sin, I am not saved, because that which is not apprehended is not saved' (*Dispute with Pyrrhus*).

Sin acts in fallen human nature, and its action begins with the human will, which is the first to be subjected to its influence. Sin can dominate a person's will, but not destroy it. This was the main point of disagreement between the Orthodox theologians and the Mono-thelite heretics in the seventh century. The latter insisted that Christ had no human will, because the will had been destroyed by sin and turned into evil. It deserved only to be rejected, and could not be accepted by Christ as part of His human nature. The Monothelites' error was to identify the will and sin, with the will indissolubly dominated by sin. For Orthodoxy, the will, although prone to sin, remains part of human nature created by God. It is not the essence of the will that has undergone malignant change, but its focus. In Christ the human will has, if you will permit me the expression, been refocused on the will of God, with both now moving in one and the same direction. It is important to note that man himself could not change the evil direction of his will – this required the divine intervention through the Son of God becoming man and hypostatically uniting human nature, including the will, with the divine nature.

In this way the will becomes a primary element in the healing of human nature from sin. With the Incarnation the human will become a channel, no longer of sin, but of grace. Just as once through the will sin came into human nature, so through it, with the Incarnation, came the salvation of man. In line with this thought are the words of the eminent Russian theologian Vladimir Lossky: 'If the will of the Son is identical with the will of the Father, then human will, which has become the will of the Word, is indeed His own will, and in this His own will is contained the whole mystery of our salvation' (*Dogmatic Theology*).

In Christ, man's will is totally aligned with the will of God. Throughout his entire life on earth, the God–man revealed the single thrust of his two wills. This was especially manifest in the agony of Gethsemane. Christ's struggle in Gethsemane has proved a stumbling block for many. People largely have been unable to accept that Christ's prayer in the Garden manifested His human will. Many have argued that Christ in the Garden of Gethsemane was merely pursuing didactic goals and wanted to demonstrate once again his human nature. But for us Orthodox it is important to understand that in the Garden of Gethsemane Christ showed not only his human nature, but also his human will, which remained subordinate to the will of God, even though the human will naturally seeks life and avoids death. Thus, in Gethsemane, Christ as a man showed his full and unconditional submission to the Divine will.

What does this Divine will consist of? In the patristic tradition, founded in Scripture, God's will is called God's plan for man, which also encompasses the moral and spiritual standards that God gave man in His commandments. Thus, the psalmist says: 'I delight to do Thy will, O my God, yea, Thy law is within my heart' (Ps. 40:8). Elsewhere the prophet David asks of God: 'Teach me to do Thy will, for Thou art my God' (Ps. 143:10). Thus, the will of God in the biblical tradition, as taken over by the Church Fathers, receives a value similar to the modern notion of moral standards which a person should strive for in order to be saved from sin.

The will of God together with the will of man are the two most important preconditions for salvation. Salvation requires the human will to be in tune with the will of God. In the patristic tradition this concordance of wills is often called synergy, i.e. co-operation between man and God. Already Origen affirmed this synergy of God and our own effort as a prerequisite for progress in bodily and spiritual virtues in his commentaries on the Psalms. This idea is picked up by many Fathers, including St Basil the Great (as in his *Letter 227* and in the *Dialogues on the Psalms*) and by St John Damascene (as in *The Life of Valaam and Joasaph*).

However, the patristic tradition talks of the synergy of man, not only with God, but also with the forces of evil. Whenever a man does evil, he is not acting in isolation, but the devil is acting with him. That is, an evil act is always committed in synergy, as is a good one, but this time the synergy is not with God, but with his opponent. This idea we find enounced, in particular, in Clement of Alexandria's *Stromata*.

In this way the human will finds itself between two wills – the divine and diabolic. The task of man is to bring our will into harmony with the will of God, and in any event not allow it to align with the will of evil forces. The direction of a person's will depends on that person himself. Man's ability to direct his will towards good or evil is referred to in contemporary language as freedom. In patristic theology, this ability is referred to with Greek terms such as *proairesis* (disposition) and *autexousion* (self-determination). This ability is discussed in detail in the treatise 'Syntagma to a politician', attributed to Athanasius of Alexandria. Even if researchers question the authorship of this work, it accurately expresses the Orthodox vision of human freedom: 'It is on the disposition (*proairesis*) that depend the punishment and honours (that man receives). (Salvation) requires as much human will and desire as it does the co-operation (*synergia*) of God – if one is absent, the other will also be slow in coming.' For the author of the *Syntagma*, man's ability for self-determination (*autexousion*), or rather to direct his will towards good or evil, is ineradicable and a guarantee of freedom. This freedom is given to him in order for him always to choose good: 'Our freedom of self-determination (*autexousion*) is a gift that can not be forced or corrupted. We have received it in order to move in two directions: good and bad. Nothing of what God has given us for our use is evil, because everything that is from God is very good. The only thing that is wrong is our abuse of our capacity for self-determination. For this reason, evil lies not in eating, but in gluttony; not in procreation, but fornication, not in the use of wine, but in drunkenness, not in money but in avarice, not in glory, but vanity. In everything we do, it is important to make correct use of what we have been given by God, avoiding all abuse. In so doing, we set ourselves above evil and become partakers in virtue.'

The ability to determine our own lives – or freedom – is God's gift, which should not be refused. But we must not abuse this gift, which has been given to us for a good purpose, not only to make choices, but to choose the good, the will of God. Freedom, as understood in the patristic tradition, demarcates that space which falls under the responsibility of man and which no external force, good nor evil, can penetrate without his permission. It is entirely up to each individual to decide whom he allows into this area of his liberty, whom he allows to operate – or more accurately, co-operate – in it: God or the devil.

Man's ability to determine the direction of his will is an important feature of his nature, according him a place of high dignity. Nevertheless, it is not in the ability to choose between good and evil that the highest value of freedom lies, but in the choice of the good, the readiness to allow divine grace into the personal space of human freedom, to give room to God in human life. This affirmation is based on the apostolic tradition of the understanding of freedom. An especially detailed development of the theology of freedom can be found in the writings of St Paul. Its essence is expressed in the well-known phrase from the Epistle to the Galatians: 'For, brethren, you have been called into liberty; only use not liberty as an occasion to the flesh, but in love serve one another' (Gal. 5:13).

Thus, the attainment of salvation and deification as the main goals of the Christian life depends on man's aligning his will with that of God. Moreover, man can choose the good will of God only freely. If he makes this choice by force, it loses its moral value. Thus, the directing of his will towards good and freedom are essential factors in man's salvation. However, despite the fact that these ideas were developed in Christian theology as early as the early centuries of the first millennium, their assimilation into the social and political life of the Christian peoples were the subject of serious conflicts and debates. From the fourth century onwards we start to see in public life a conviction that the moral development of man can be achieved through political means. In all likelihood, this was associated with an optimistic understanding of the possibilities of earthly institutions to correct the human soul. For example, St Augustine, who in his diocese was warring against the Donatist schism, wrote: 'I succumbed to the facts. Bishops pelted me with examples, not only of individual persons, but of entire cities, previously dominated by Donatism and in which Orthodoxy now reigns. Especially notable in this regard is my own city, the residents of which used to be mainly Donatists, and which now under the influence of the emperor has turned to Orthodoxy and with such hatred towards the Donatists, that one cannot believe that the city was ever Donatist.' This case of the use of political power in overcoming Donatism illustrates the dominance at the time, both in the West and the East, of a particular image of the role of government in the maintenance of morality.

Let us briefly consider how this idea developed in Western Europe, since the forms of church and social life that arose here were later to play a crucial role in the emergence and formation of ideas emphasising the importance of human freedom. Following the collapse of the Western Roman Empire in the late fifth century, the Roman Church remained the only cohesive organisation in the 'post-Roman' area to preserve the continuity of the previous great state. In the political turmoil that prevailed in the former Western empire for several centuries, the Roman Church gradually took upon itself the functions of a State institution. This ultimately led to the creation of the Papal States in the eighth century and to the emergence of the ideology that justified the rule of ecclesiastical authority in political matters. Under the so-called concept of the 'two swords', the Roman Church started to use the mechanisms of government to organise its internal life: to impose taxes, to defend its rights against the secular authorities by force, to conduct campaigns of conquest, to regulate the private lives of its flock through terrestrial mechanisms. In the twelfth century it created the Inquisition that in the sixteenth century turned into a punitive tool against dissent.

Representatives of the Renaissance and the Enlightenment, and later revolutionary leaders put forward the idea of freedom in a secularised form, giving it an anti-Catholic and anti-Christian character, because for them the Catholic Church was the pillar of regimes they considered tyrannical. If the Reformation remained within the scope of Christian values, the subsequent movements for freedom, as a rule, rejected an important part of the Christian message on freedom – that of moral responsibility before God. The result has been a falling into the other extreme – that of the absolutisation of personal freedom.

In the East, the situation differed from the Western norm of Church-State relations, in a manner more consistent with the patristic conception of man. The key document of this approach is the sixth *novella* of Emperor Justinian, resulting from the codification of Roman law undertaken under that emperor in the mid-sixth century. In this document kingship and priesthood are viewed as two equal gifts of God. This statement leaves little room for the dispute, which raged for centuries in the West, as to who is superior, Church or State, and who must obey whom. In the East the idea of a balance between the two institutions was formulated. According to the sixth *novella*, the task of the State is to ensure the implementation of God's law in public life and the protection of the faith. The Church is responsible for spiritual matters and supports the State in carrying out its functions. The underlying idea here is of a certain degree of autonomy of both Church and State, but at the same time of mutual support.

In Byzantium the patriarch had a special right of 'lamentations', that is of pleading the cause of disenfranchised people in front of the authorities. Inevitably the history of Byzantium is uneven in this respect. Not every patriarch or cleric dared take issue with the emperor or powerful dignitaries. Indeed, it is difficult to point to any era in which the ideal of harmonious and symphonic relations between Church and State was implemented in full. However, the concept itself of an equilibrium between State power and the authority of the Church always existed in Byzantium.

With the adoption of Christianity, Rus and Russia relied on the Byzantine model of Church-State relations. As in Byzantium, so to in Russia, real national tragedies have come about whenever the one side has sought to bring the other under its thumb. We recall here both Ivan the Terrible's attempt to subjugate the Church to the State and the activities of Patriarch Nikon, who sought to elevate the role of the Church and its primate in the country's political life to excessive levels. Both paths proved disastrous for the Church and for society. However, these violations of the principle of symphony were associated with particular historical figures, but did not signify rejection by Russia of the concept itself. A radical change in the life of the nation did take place, however, with the rejection in principle of this norm in the early eighteenth century, and the borrowing of the Protestant model of Church-State relations, subordinating the Church to the State. From then on we witness an increasing gap between the Church and society, the Church and the intelligentsia, the Church and the political elite. The State, having lost the counterweight of an independent Church, gradually develops an extensive mechanism of enforcement and regulation, which suppresses individual liberty.

By importing alien models of Church-State relations onto its soil, Russia created conditions for the spread of the same shortcomings of social life that were typical of Western Europe. On this followed, quite naturally, the perpetration of Enlightenment and revolutionary ideas and the absolutisation of individual liberty.

In the twentieth century, both in the West and in Russia, we witnessed a further development of liberalism, and in a very dangerous direction, with the idea of freedom promoted solely in the direction of freedom of choice, and hence of the possibility to choose in favour of evil. This led to a radical rejection of the normative significance of tradition, especially religious tradition, and to the absolute right of an individual to determine what is good and what is evil. In practice this absolutisation turned into moral and axiological relativism and found its clearest expression in the authoritarian regimes of the twentieth century, with the place of the individual taken by the political party and its leader, and in post-modern individualism, where individual liberty from the moral norms of tradition is supported at the legislative level.

Today people talk about freedom as never before. But it is today that we are seeing the development of processes that pose a threat to personal freedom. Considering freedom to be the highest value, the State and the international community impose as law socio-political norms which are contrary to the life of believers who belong to traditional religions. On the one hand, no one encroaches on another person's privacy, but at the societal level believers are increasingly being forced to accept a norm of life that is contrary to their beliefs. Soon, this may lead to a situation in which Christians or any other believers will be unable to hold many socially important positions and undertake many activities because they will be required to do things that cannot be done without betraying their faith and without committing sin.

The most striking example of the possibility of such a scenario was recently demonstrated at European Union level, where the European Parliament rejected the candidacy of Italian politician Rocco Buttiglione as Commissioner for Justice and Home Affairs of the European Commission because of his expressed aversion to homosexuality as a norm of interpersonal relations. Another case involved a former mayor of New York, Mr Giuliani. In formulating his position on abortion, even when he was mayor of an American metropolis, he said that as a Christian he was against abortion, but as mayor he had to support it, because this was the will of the majority of the city's residents.

Can a Christian be active in the public sphere, if the fact of his occupying a post in government, business and community organisations requires actions that are inconsistent with his religious beliefs? Norms prescribing such actions are emerging today in many countries around the world. Similar steps are also being taken at the international level. Russia, and other countries in which the Russian Church carries out its mission, will tomorrow be required to adopt and implement these rules being adopted in Western countries today.

Another problem now is that a mechanism of control is gradually being developed over the activities of the individual at both national and international level. We introduce new methods of identification which involve the collection and storage of data on people's individual personality traits, consumption patterns and income. All this is connected with the desire to curb illegal migration, crime, terrorism, and also regulate the collection of taxes. In short, the development of control in this area is intended to ensure compliance with legal requirements. But against the background of the introduction of international norms and national legislation that are contrary to moral norms, believers are beginning to ask a totally logical question: 'Will not one fine day these controls be used to verify implementation of these norms?' And if today people can express their disagreement with legislation that is contrary to their faith, then tomorrow their observance of these rules will be monitored by means of increasingly sophisticated systems of control.

Aware of all these problems and their importance for the fate of Christianity and the Church, the Russian Orthodox Church believes, as expressed in its document *The Basis of the Social Concept of the Russian Orthodox Church*, that Christians should not retreat into their own enclosed circle. Such a retreat does not contribute to the mission of the Church, called by its Saviour to preach the Word of God to the whole earth. The Church has therefore continued to be present in the modern world and to witness to its position. At the same time, however, it is important for its members to be aware of their otherness in relation to the world in which they live and work. Following this logic, the Russian Church is actively developing its relations with the State, society and international organisations such as the European Union, Council of Europe, the United Nations and others.

Two millennia of Christian history show that the conflicts and clashes that took place in the socio-political sphere of the Christian nations, took place within the framework of Christian values, even if at times the adherents of one party to the conflict lost or denied their connection with Christianity. Freedom and morality are two categories of patristic anthropology. But just as important is the way these two categories are inextricably linked in patristic understanding. Absolutisation of either one of these categories at the expense of the other inevitably leads to public tragedies.

What the Orthodox Church is preaching today is an insistence on the interdependence and interrelation of these two categories in the spirit of patristic theology. Indeed, the human right to life, to fair trial, to work and the like are important elements of public and political life, because they are based on Christian ideas. But equally important are the observance of moral principles and their proper reflection in the development of law and policy. In bearing this message to the modern world the Orthodox Church can draw on a broad coalition of traditional Christian churches, traditional religions and conservative social movements.

In conclusion, I would stress just how important the moral choices of contemporary humanity are for the future of the world. Man's choice always contains an eschatological perspective, because on whether he takes the path of life or death depends the course of human history and its ultimate outcome. From the Book of Revelation we know that at the end of human history, the Antichrist will reign and the establishment of his kingdom will be possible only because people choose evil over good. Each of us, choosing evil, hastens the arrival of the Antichrist, and by staying true to the good, prevents him from prevailing. Of course, the crown of human history is not the kingdom of the Antichrist, but the glorious coming of Christ and the universal resurrection of the dead. Christ's second coming will be the fulfilment of the aspirations of all those who in life sought to do good and avoid evil, those who chose God's will and not that of the devil, who did not abuse their freedom but used it purposefully – that is, co-operating with the good will of God.

Chapter 5

NO FREEDOM WITHOUT MORAL RESPONSIBILITY

From a meeting with journalists from the Literaturnaya Gazeta *weekly, no. 45–46, 2–8 November 2005*

The most important questions facing us today are, it seems to me, those concerning the meaning of life. There is nothing new about them, but they have become particularly acute in our today's world. In this respect, CDP leader Angela Merkel, with whom I had a long talk during my visit to Germany in February 2005, put forward an engaging idea. She told me that the once incredibly popular slogan of 'A Better Life' is no longer meaningful for Germans, which is why she is keen to address a different message to the nation, focusing on the spiritual aspects of human existence.

The same problems concern me too. Every reform and every revolution, as we all know all too well, has been undertaken for the sake of a 'better', that is, a full, well-provided-for and comfortable, life. For seventy years, millions in our country lived for such a 'bright future', denying themselves everything, and many even dying for it. All this for an idea that has proved unattainable in real life. The socialist experiment failed not because ours was the 'wrong' socialism, nor because the mechanism of economic management was too cumbersome, nor because of a lack of competition, nor for any such similar reason.

But why then did it fail? For me, as a believer, because there was no blessing of God; because Soviet ideology was not just atheistic, that is without God, but expressly anti-God.

Today, the economic vector of government policy has changed, but look more closely and you will find that the direction people give to their lives is not fundamentally different: their goal is still to live better, meaning for most of them to be richer and more successful. And that's all!

It is my profound conviction that, on the basis of Russia's historical experience, we, as no one else, can address ourselves to the world with a unique message. This is that building a welfare state will never make humanity happy if this welfare is sought outside the context of man's spiritual needs.

This is a complex and multi-dimensional topic, not easily reduced to a single conceptual level. But the first thing to which I would like to direct your attention and to reflect upon with you is the inter-dependence of human freedom and moral responsibility. Can human freedom exist without moral responsibility, and does a person who has no freedom have any moral responsibility?

The age of the Enlightenment declared man to be the centre of the universe. This man was viewed also as sinless from birth. Rousseau, for instance, set forth a theory of education based on a natural development of the inclinations placed in man by nature, free from the influence of social institutions, and by definition without any concept of sinfulness. And if people are indeed born immaculate, it is only right and proper that they be given full freedom to realise their human potential. Hence the idea of the absolute value of human rights and liberties that has prevailed until now in Western liberal society. The French Revolution mainstreamed this political paradigm, from whence it determined the political thought of the European nations and in the twentieth century went on to form the basis of international organisations. Ask today's European bureaucrats in Brussels and Strasbourg how they see their task, and they will tell you that in the first place it is to protect human rights and freedoms, because all existing troubles are caused by the failure of individual states to observe these rights.

I too am convinced of the need to protect human rights and freedoms. But I am also convinced that human beings are not born sinless. Even leaving aside the theological aspect, and Christian anthropology with its teaching on the corruption of human nature as a consequence of the Fall, simple observation tells us that, regrettably, every child inherits not only the physical but also the moral vices of its parents. The latest genetic advances have only re-confirmed this depressing truth. This means that the 'liberation' of the individual, his free development without any correction by society, will lead also to the liberation of the dark 'Dionysian' principle, as the Greeks called it, present in every person. This is a dead-end – the way to destruction for our civilisation. It is this that makes the liberal principle, which tells us that 'my freedom should not restrict the freedom of another person', so very dangerous, if it is the only restraining principle.

Many times our opponents tell us that 'you Orthodox simply have a latent allergy to the very theme of rights and freedoms'. No, not at all. In the Soviet time our Church suffered like no one else from oppression by the authorities. Moreover, the very idea of rights and freedoms is based on the Christian understanding of the human being as the image of God, and thus the high dignity of the human person. But if we separate the task of observing and protecting human rights from the moral responsibility of the individual before God and his fellow men, then we condemn humanity to the unleashing of the passions, to an upsurge of instincts that can easily turn society into a pack of wolves.

Hence the question: are these two mindsets, Christian and liberal, mutually reconcilable? Yes, but it is a rather complicated task. Success can be achieved when rights and freedoms are combined with traditional ethical values as presented by religion and the national awareness of peoples. You certainly are aware of the debates going on today in the West concerning same-sex marriages. It is precisely this fundamental theme of inter-relationship between human ethics and freedom which is in play here. Today there is a demand that same-sex couples should enjoy the same rights as normal families. What can we oppose to this tendency? Only the absolute ethical norm as secured in the ethical teaching of the Church.

But look at what is happening now. Religion in the West has been ousted to the realm of private life almost as successfully as it was in our country under the Soviet power. You can be a believer only in church or at home. Your Christian convictions cannot motivate your actions in social life. Take, for instance, the refusal of the members of the

European Parliament to confirm the appointment of Italian Rocco Buttiglione as European Commissioner only because he, being a good Catholic, called homosexual activity a sin. And now Jerusalem mayor Uri Lupoliansky is facing legal prosecution for banning a gay pride parade in the Holy City – that is, for banning open propaganda for sin.

At the same time the secular world believes it has the right to interfere in the internal affairs of churches. In some European countries the question is being raised of the need to require churches by law to ordain openly proclaimed homosexuals, and all this for the sake of observing the 'human right' to commit a sin that destroys human nature.

In our days the notion of truth has been ousted from the public consciousness, to be replaced by a 'pluralism of opinions'. In this system all ideas, all views, are considered to have equal rights and to be equally entitled to express themselves. Let me cite as an example the polemic that took place in the mass media surrounding the Second World War 60th victory anniversary celebrations. At that time, active attempts were made to put on an equal footing the feat of the people who stopped the Fascist onslaught and the betrayal of those who killed their own brothers with German weapons in their hands. This is only one example of where truth and falsehood are placed on an equal footing, where the hierarchy of values is replaced by a free market of ideas working according to the laws of supply and demand, demand in this case determined by the moral state of a 'consumer' – the lower the moral level, the more popular the most repulsive ideas.

But what enables us to distinguish here between truth and falsehood? Only the frame of reference established by Divine Revelation and safeguarded by the Tradition of the Church, absolute because it has divine authority. A believer cherishes it in his heart, and no television, no newspaper, can shake him. And here we have a paradox: it is precisely within the Christian Church, during the Reformation, that the struggle with this understanding of the criteria of truth was initiated. In 1517, precisely 400 years before the Russian Revolution, a revolution occurred in Christian awareness in the

West. Its focal point was the rejection of the absolute authority of the Church in interpreting Holy Scriptures. From then on, one could say: 'I have the Holy Spirit in me, and my understanding of the truth of the gospel is no way inferior to that of the Holy Fathers, the Councils and the Church.' The inevitable consequence of this is first doctrinal and then moral relativism. Modern history is testimony to this. But this is, I repeat, a dead-end street – something that sensible leaders of the civilised world have begun to grasp.

Unless we recover the ability to distinguish between good and evil, which we need to be able to do in order to maintain our bearings in the unlimited expanse of modern civilisation, any hope of a different, more promising future is impossible.

> Anatoly Salutskiy, writer: 'In the perestroika years the so-called "common human values" began to be actively imposed on us. ... But don't you think these "common human values" are really Western values, and, however respectable in themselves, are foreign to us? Is not their imposition on Russia basically a continuation of the centuries-old attempt, since the fall of Byzantium, to deprive us of of our national identity, national moral qualities, etc.?'

When Mikhail S. Gorbachev first pronounced the words 'common human values', I understood that the dominion of Marxism, at least in Russia, had come to an end. Marxist ethics reject any idea of common moral values. Moral is everything that serves the proletariat – this was its basic assumption. But the tasks faced by the proletariat vary in various ages. This means that moral categories also change with time. Moreover, the proletariat and the bourgeoisie as its perpetual enemy could never arrive at any shared understanding of morality. And now, all of a sudden, the leader of the world's largest communist party and the head of its most powerful communist state was speaking about values common to all people, regardless of their class and social and property status; that is, *de facto* recognising the existence of a universal categorical moral imperative! This is tanta-mount to the recognition of the existence of God, because it is only the Absolute – that is, God – who can be the source of absolute morality. In this sense the use of the term 'common human values' is quite admissible if understood as values instilled in man by his Creator and therefore common to people in the USA, Russia and Papua-New Guinea.

But what is meant today by common human values are in fact the values of the Enlightenment. Formulated as the outcome of a specific socio-political development and its philosophical underpinning in Western Europe, they are rooted in the heathen idea of man as measure of all things, albeit incorporating some ideas of Protestantism and Jewish philosophy as taught in European universities after the dispersion of the Jews. The result is that neither Catholic ethical doctrine, nor the basic provisions of Orthodox axiology, nor the ethics of traditional Islam or Judaism, are duly reflected in this system, which is the intellectual product of a specific civilisational model.

We treat it with respect and are ready to enter into dialogue with its representatives, but only on equal footing. But today we are allowed to speak and preach whatever we wish only if we do not encroach on the fundamentals of this worldview. Its adepts have appropriated the right to assess all and sundry on the basis on their own scale of moral values, and are eager to fit all the diversity of the world into the Procrustean bed of their own standards.

It is my profound conviction that Russia should advocate the idea of a multi-polar world. These poles should not be exclusively political, as diplomats would understand it. Reality demands that we recognise the indisputable fact that several cultures today coexist in parallel. They are rooted in different religious experiences, including, paradoxically, even the rejection of religion – that is, atheism. Can we find some docking points in them? For me we can. If we all agree on the existence of a common ethical framework of reference, these docking points will appear on their own. Russia itself offers a unique example of such unity in diversity. Our history and the contemporary situation witness to the coexistence of East and West, Christianity and Islam, religiosity and secularism. And Russia can become a prototype of a new world order, based not on impersonal unity within standards imposed by force – which can lead only to civilisational catastrophe – but on a harmonious combination based on an externally diverse but essentially unified perception of absolute moral values.

> Alexander Tsipko, political commentator of Literaturnaya Gazeta: '... Yes, I am fully aware that the idea of ecumenism in the form of unification of Christian confessions into a single whole, as advocated by Vladimir Solovyev, is a dangerous thing. The different Christian confessions are guardians of vital civilisational and cultural codes and patterns, and if these are destroyed in the search for Christian unity, the whole of human culture can break down. But even so I do not understand why Christian churches are unaware of the dangers you point to and do nothing to oppose this liberal anthropocentrism which is actually ousting Christianity from Europe. Why do Christian churches do nothing to develop a common policy for saving not just Christianity but the common human morality and culture? Is it possible to do something to solve this problem?'

Your humble servant was granted a private audience by Pope Benedict XVI the day after his enthronement. We spoke precisely about this. The Catholic and the Orthodox Churches in today's world are natural – and, it seems, the only – allies in the tough struggle between representatives of secular liberalism infected with the bacillus of self-destruction, and bearers of the forward-looking idea of human salvation. We can join with Catholics in defending Christian values. We already have experience of working together here. During the preparation of the draft European Constitution we entered into intensive dialogue with the Catholic Church and reached mutual understanding on this problem.

Chapter 6

HUMAN RIGHTS AND MORAL RESPONSIBILITY

Address to the 10th World Council of Russian People, 'Faith, Man, Land. Russia's Mission in the Twenty-first Century', Moscow, 4 April 2006

For Russia and her peoples in the twenty-first century, questions of science and technology, economics and social development will remain of primary importance. It is clear, however, that the energy necessary for any human endeavour can be drawn only from the spiritual realm. This means that the successful implementation of these tasks will very much depend on how they are integrated into the spiritual parameters of the civilisation that is particular to Russia and to the entire Russian world. Moreover, relations with the external world, that is with other civilisations, above all Western, will remain an important factor in the development of Russian civilisation as a whole. It is here that the ideological foundations of these relations acquire special significance. In the case of Western civilisation we are dealing with human rights and dignity. The Orthodox tradition, which has formed Russian culture, has to respond to this challenge, otherwise Russian society both at home and abroad will become a marginalised phenomenon in the modern world.

Since 1991, the countries that emerged from the break-up of the Soviet Union have established human rights and liberties as the central norm in social and political relations. No one questions this choice. On the contrary, political and social leaders constantly affirm their faithfulness to these principles.

However, over the last few years tendencies have developed in the area of human rights which are viewed by believers as two-faced, to say the least. On the one hand, human rights exist for the good of mankind. We must not forget that it is thanks to their influence on public opinion in the countries of the former socialist bloc that the Russian Orthodox Church and other religious communities in Eastern Europe were freed from the shackles of atheism. Moreover, human rights combat various abuses, humiliation and evils committed against the person in society.

But, on the other hand, we have become witnesses to the fact that the human rights concept is used to cover up lies, falsehood and insults against religious and national values. Moreover, the catalogue of human rights and freedoms is gradually being augmented by ideas which conflict not only with the Christian but also with the traditional moral understanding of the person. This is alarming, since behind human rights stands the coercive power of the State, which can compel people to commit sin, tolerate it, or allow it to take place through banal conformism.

All of this moves the issue of human rights from the purely political realm into one that affects the lives and fates of people – something that we would refer to in Church parlance as 'the salvation of the person'. It should be remembered that soteriology, or the doctrine of salvation, lies at the heart of the Christian message. It is thus important for the believing person to answer the following questions. Do the acceptance of and adherence to the norms of the concept of human rights in their current form in international and national law contradict God's plan for humankind? To what degree can human rights foster or hinder the life of the Christian and of the believer in general? Today, members of the Russian Orthodox Church are called on to ponder these questions, on which the common mind of the Church needs to be bought to bear also.

It is widely held that human rights are a universal norm, that there can be no specific Orthodox, Islamic, Buddhist, Russian or American concept of human rights, since this would introduce relativity into the understanding of human rights, thus considerably restricting their functioning in international life. This is the thinking of many politicians and public leaders. Indeed, one can understand the desire to preserve the universal character of the concept of rights and liberties, not dependent on any variables. In fact, Orthodox people do not object to the existence of certain universal rules of behaviour in the modern world. But these rules must be truly universal. Can human rights as set forth today really lay claim to such universality?

The point is that this concept was generated and developed in Western countries, with their unique historical and cultural destiny. In these countries it successfully took root, but also revealed its shortcomings. Population decline and asocial and amoral behaviour (i.e. everything that has become a social problem in the West), is often explained precisely by excessive individualism. But does this mean that Western standards of human happiness are applicable to all countries and all cultures? Other civilisations also have their positive experience of social life. Why is it that they are not entitled to speak their mind? Of course they have such a right. This is the right of every people.

In order for Russian civilisation to speak its word on human rights, it is necessary to conduct a careful analysis of this concept in its present state. Above all, discussion is needed of the philosophical ideas that lie at the foundation of the concept of human rights and thus affect its development and application.

Central to the modern concept of human rights is the idea of 'human dignity'. Human dignity is the main motive for and justification of the existence of rights and liberties. It is for the protection of human dignity that particular rights and liberties have been formulated. In the historical development of Western countries, the list of rights and liberties has kept growing, covering ever new areas of social life. Political, economic, cultural and social rights have developed. New facets of human dignity have appeared. In recent years, the problems of sexual relations, the status of human life and bioethics have grown increasingly acute. In this way a new generation of human rights has arisen as people continue to define the essence of man. Therefore it is important today as never before to try to clarify what human dignity is.

In various languages, the word 'dignity' has always been linked to a person's social position. To act according to one's dignity meant to act in accordance with the rights and duties that accompanied one's social status. The very word 'dignity' means 'that which deserves respect and honour, that which is of great significance and value'. Thus, two meanings are united in this word. Firstly, that a certain subject is of value. Secondly, dignity signifies the conformity of the life of the subject to this value. For the Orthodox tradition, establishing the correlation between these two aspects of dignity is very important.

In Christian culture, the value of the person is unshakeable and objective. The person is part of God's creation, of which the Lord said: 'it is good' (Gen. 1:25). Investing particular value in man, God made him stand out from the rest of creation, for in the book of Genesis it is written that God blessed the first human beings after creating them (Gen. 1:28). This means that God wished good to the human race, and that His wishes are unchanging. Thus, the value of the person is defined by his value in the eyes of God. This is confirmed by the presence in human nature of the seal of God Himself – His image. We know of this also from the Book of Genesis (1:26).

Even the Fall of man did not diminish this value. God did not destroy man who had walked away from Him, but did and continues to do everything to make possible his return to his original calling – i.e. for man's salvation. The fact of the Incarnation of the Son of God is an especially important testimony to the fact that man was not forsaken by God after the Fall. The Lord Jesus Christ took on human nature and cleansed it from sin. The Incarnation is testimony of the pre-eminent value of human nature, assumed by Jesus Christ and brought into the life of the Triune God.

After his creation, man not only possessed value in the eyes of God, he also reflected this value in his life. In other words, he had dignity, and his task was to grow in this dignity. The book of Genesis tells of how God placed man on this path, blessing him to cultivate the created world. Commenting on the biblical account of human nature, some Fathers of the Church have pointed to the simultaneous presence of static and dynamic elements in it. The presence of the image of God in human nature signifies his intransient value, while 'likeness' signifies the task of developing this value. St John

Damascene writes: 'The expression "in the image of" refers to the capabilities of the mind and freedom, while "in the likeness of" signifies the degree of similarity to God in virtue, inasmuch as it is possible for man'. Thus, man's task in life was to become ever more similar to God and thus grow in dignity.

The Fall did not change this task, but made it impossible for man without God's help. Having desired to reach perfection without God, humankind lost its tie with the source that had nourished its creative activity. What happened? Although human nature continued to be of value in the eyes of God due to the presence in it of God's image, man ceased to act in keeping with the value inherent in his nature and thus lost his dignity to a significant degree. Man's goal now was to regain his lost dignity and increase it. In this light, not all human actions can be considered as reflecting the norms established by God at Creation, from which it follows that there are forms of behaviour that cannot be included in the catalogue of human rights and liberties.

The most important aspect of the process of restoring man to his dignity is the direction of his will. Man is endowed with freedom, without which even God's help in correcting behaviour is impossible. Thanks to his freedom man has a choice: to adhere to the good and thus regain his dignity or to choose evil and thus diminish his dignity. Even in contemporary humanistic thought, there is the understanding that man is constantly faced with the choice between good and evil actions. There are thus norms of behaviour which are encouraged by legislation, as well as actions that are subject to punishment. However, the difference between secular humanism and religious tradition lies in what they take as their authority in defining good and evil.

For some reason, the idea has taken root in modern Western thought since the time of Jean-Jacques Rousseau that it is sufficient to grant freedom and rights to the individual for him to choose invariably what is good and beneficial for him. Therefore, no external authorities should point out to him what is good and what is bad. The person himself should define the norms for his behaviour. This is known as the moral autonomy of the person. This autonomy can be limited only by the autonomy of another person. The notion of sin is absent from this ideology, characterised by a pluralism of opinions. The individual may choose for himself any variant of behaviour, but on condition that his behaviour does not limit the freedom of other people. The regrettable consequence of this anthropocentric approach is that many countries today are building a social system which is lenient toward sin and distances itself from the task of promoting the moral perfection of the person. Society, including ours, finds itself facing a cynical substitution. The admissibility of immoral behaviour is justified by the teaching on human dignity which, as I have mentioned above, has religious roots.

And man indeed possesses complete autonomy to accept or reject rules. God endowed him with the capability of self-determination. This is the freedom before which God Himself stops. I would like to stress that Christianity cannot contest this affirmation in the dialogue with secular humanism. It only challenges the affirmation of the capability of the individual autonomously to make choices that will always correspond to his real good. The individual, in a state of sin after the Fall, cannot always clearly distinguish by himself the good from the bad. This is not because he is foolish, but because his reason, will and feelings can be influenced by sin, and he may make mistakes in defining goals for his life. The tragedy is that the very notions of good and evil remain in the person, but he is not always able to distinguish clearly between the two. God helps man to maintain this ability to discern through His Revelation, which contains a well-known code of moral rules accepted by practically all religious traditions.

For the believer who is aware of the problem of the self-determination of the will, the claim that moral anthropocentrism is a universal principle that should regulate social and personal activity gives cause for doubt. Conscience is an important criterion that helps distinguish between good and evil. It is not by chance that folk wisdom calls the conscience the voice of God, for the moral law placed by God into human nature is known in the voice of conscience. But the voice of conscience can be stifled by sin. Therefore, when making moral choices one must also be guided by external criteria, above all by the commandments given by God. In this respect it is an important fact that in the Decalogue all main world religions are in accord with each other in their definition of good and evil. The religious tradition thus contains a criterion for discerning good from evil. From the perspective of this tradition, the following cannot be accepted as normative: mockery of sacred things, abortion, homosexual activity, euthanasia and other actions that are actively advocated today by the concept of human rights. Unfortunately, today the absolutisation of the State characteristic of modernity is being replaced by the absolutisation of the sovereignty of the individual and his rights without moral responsibility. This absolutisation can destroy the foundations of modern civilisation and lead to its downfall. It is a well-established fact that the trampling on of the moral law has led many powerful civilisations to destruction and their disappearance from the face of the earth. Humankind cannot live outside a moral context. No laws can help us keep society viable or put an end to corruption, the misuse of power, the break-up of the family, the abandoning of children, the reduction of the birthrate, the destruction of nature, militant nationalism, xenophobia or the mockery of religious sentiments. To paraphrase a well-known saying of Dostoevsky, if a person does not see that he is committing sin, then everything is allowed.

Acts of cruelty have shocked our society recently. Why is this happening in our country? I would say: because we have forgotten about morality and about how we must make efforts to preserve it. The language of moral norms is understandable for everybody. Morality is one and indivisible. If, pointing to the rights and liberties of the individual, we make way for sin and do not stop manifestations of human barbarism, when we allow icons to be chopped to pieces in Manezh Square in the centre of Moscow, when we allow the exhibition 'Beware of Religion' to be held and let people elsewhere mock the sentiments of believers through caricatures, then why are we appalled at the appearance of people willing to commit murder based on national and religious identity? The instinct of destruction, when it comes to the surface, does not spare anyone – neither believers in a synagogue, nor children with a different skin colour. These are all links in one chain. Our society should understand that it is impossible to achieve respect for people of different nationalities and faiths without re-examining its attitude toward morality in the mass media, school, politics, the economy and culture.

No one contests that a society in which the individual is disdained, in which the State and the collective possess all rights over the person, is unstable and inhumane. But societies in which human rights become an instrument for the emancipation of the instincts, in which the notions of good and evil are confused and driven out by the idea of moral autonomy and pluralism, become equally inhumane. Such societies lose their mechanisms of moral influence on the personality. In civilised society − let us call it so − the balance between these polarities must be maintained. It should base itself on the understanding that each person by nature possesses unchanging value, and at the same time that everyone is called on to grow in dignity and bear civic responsibility before the law and moral responsibility for his actions.

All this poses a very important question: how can we guarantee the free choice of the person while supporting the moral direction of this choice? In doing so both human efforts and God's help play an important role.

Of course, we should give first place to God's help, which is granted to the individual in religious life. Communion with God helps a person to distinguish good from evil and gain the strength to make the choice in favour of the good. In prayer, the sacramental life of the Church and good works is accomplished the uniting of man with God, which brings with itself strengthening in the doing of good. This is why for the believer religious life and all notions associated with it acquire primary significance. Along with freedom, it becomes the main condition for the successful life of the person both on earth and in eternity.

But human efforts are also important. They should be directed toward a shaping of social relations which, on the one hand, can guarantee the freedom of the individual, and on the other hand can help him adhere to moral norms. It would probably be incorrect to establish criminal responsibility for gambling, euthanasia and homosexual activity, but we also cannot accept them as a legislative norm and, what is more important, as a moral norm approved of by society.

What happens when laws are passed that officially allow such forms of behaviour? They no longer remain the practice of a small minority that has already made its choice. These laws become the foundation for the unhindered propaganda of such forms of behaviour in society. And, since sin is attractive, it quickly infects large segments of society, especially if large sums of money are put into its propaganda and advanced methods of influencing consciousness are employed.

Such is the case with homosexuality. The resolution adopted in January of this year by the European Parliament requires schools to educate pupils in the spirit of acceptance of homosexuality and even fixes a day in the year dedicated to the fight against homophobia. What has been the result of this? Not only is society called on to respect the lifestyle of a certain minority, but it is required to undertake propaganda of the homosexual lifestyle as a certain norm. As a result this propaganda becomes a stumbling-block for those who would otherwise fight against this vice and raise normal, fully-fledged families.

We can also cite an example from our own life in Russia. Today, in many cities, gambling houses and casinos have appeared like mush-rooms after a rainstorm. Naturally, nobody forces anyone to visit these institutions, but their advertising is so intrusive and the passion for gambling so easily aroused that today we have to deal with real family tragedies. Fathers, mothers and children gamble away the little money they have and leave their families without a penny. People come to church and weep because of the break-up of their families. As a result the freedom of the gambling business, not reasonably restricted in any way, is destroying society.

I have tried to mention the dangers that arise for believers when an approach to human rights unbalanced by moral norms lays claims to being the only true understanding of these rights. According to this logic, all other traditions should be silent and submit. I am not making this up, and I am not exaggerating the dictatorial attitude of the adherents of such a reading of human rights. This approach is already moving forward confidently in contemporary international legislation. Thus, in 2005, the Parliamentary Assembly of the Council of Europe adopted a resolution entitled 'Women and Religion in

Europe', which states that 'the freedom of religion is limited by human rights'. This affirmation subjugates religious life to human rights. If the former does not correspond to a certain understanding of freedom, it must be changed. For the believing person this sounds like a call to deriding God's will for the sake of human notions.

In saying so I would like to stress that it would nevertheless be unjust to downplay the very concept of human rights. What we have here is a situation in which a certain philosophy shared by a small circle of people is hiding behind the mask of human rights. According to this philosophy, if women are not ordained to the priesthood or episcopacy of a certain religious community, the community should be subject to punishment by the State and derision by society. However, for the believer the norms of religious tradition are more authoritative than earthly laws. If this militant spirit of the secular humanistic approach, which may eventually enter international law, is not eliminated today, conflict will automatically arise. Thank God, in the case of the Council of Europe's resolution, its requirements do not have legal consequences, but they do create a certain climate in public opinion.

There is one more liberal affirmation that is laying claims to universality. It states that human rights should prevail over the interests of society. This was repeated in the following words in the UNESCO declaration on the universal principles of bioethics of 2005: 'The interests and good of the individual should have priority over those of science and society' (ch. 3, par. 2). It is quite clear that this affirmation is positive when it concerns State and public decision-making affecting the life and welfare of individual citizens. Society should cherish every life, every person.

However, this approach becomes very dangerous when the individual begins to base his behaviour on his own interests as having priority over those of society. This only stimulates egoism and individualism. Orthodoxy has always advocated self-sacrificing love towards one's neighbour, and thus towards one's family, local community and homeland. It is important to be able to put aside egoism in favour of another person. Therefore, in our opinion, it would be correct that liberties and rights always be balanced by social solidarity.

Orthodox believers are ready to accept the choice of world-view of other nations, but they cannot keep silent when norms contradicting the foundations of Orthodox faith are imposed upon them. I think we can say that this view is shared by Muslims, Buddhists, Jews and people of other faiths. In order to avoid conflict in today's world, it is necessary to engage in an intensive effort to harmonise various world-views. General principles for the life of the world community should be worked out jointly by various civilisations.

How then can contemporary society be organised in such a way that human rights might be harmoniously combined with morality?

Firstly, legislation should be sensitive to the moral norms that predominate in society. It is not for State structures to define what is good and what is bad, but at the same time legislation should reflect the moral norms shared by the majority of society. If society feels that arousing the passion for drinking and exploiting the sexual instinct for commercial purposes are unacceptable, there should be appropriate legislation forbidding the advertising of them.

Secondly, the vacuum of moral education in our society must be filled. Freedom and rights are a significant achievement of human civilisation, but we must also prepare citizens to make use of these rights, with proper regard for moral norms. The State, in close co-operation with social institutions of moral education, including schools and, of course, the country's religious communities, should undertake this preparation. This implies that the State should take it upon itself to work out legislation governing the access of religious organisations to public educational structures, social service, health and the armed forces.

In doing so, all religious communities in the country should labour in these areas according to their representation in society. Very important here is that competition in mission work be categorically rejected in order to avoid inter-religious confrontation, to which battling between religious organisations for new adherents inevitably leads.

Finally, the attitude of the mass media toward the harmonisation of human rights with morality is very important today. They should give positive examples of the use of freedom. How can a person make moral use of his or her freedom when television proposes consumerism, violence, debauchery, gambling and other vices as a successful way of life? To justify themselves, people working in television and in mass media as a whole say that such products are in demand and sell well. Nobody will argue that vice sells easily, since it is easily accepted by fallen human nature, which tends toward sin. From ancient times this has gone under the heading of temptation.

However, it is not true that modern man demands only vice. He seeks happiness, peace, true love and other virtues. It is astonishing that today old Soviet, newer Russian and foreign films dealing with serious questions of life are in great demand.

Orthodox people are willing to accept human rights norms and work toward strengthening them, but on the condition that these norms promote the perfection of the individual, not the justification of his sinful condition. The task of the concept of human rights is to defend the value of the person and foster the development of his dignity. In this we see the most important and the only possible purpose of this concept from the Christian perspective.

It is wrong and sinful when the rights of nations and ethnic groups to their own religion, language and culture are violated, and the freedom of religion and rights of believers to their own way of life are limited, when crimes of religion and nationality are committed. Our moral sensitivities cannot remain silent when people are subjected to the whims of civil servants and employers, when soldiers are helpless before hazing, when children and the elderly become the objects of mockery in social institutions. The manipulation of consciousness by destructive sects, and the involvement of young people in crime, slavery, prostitution, drug abuse and gambling addiction are also inadmissible and must be rejected. We must resist such phenomena as diminishing human dignity. Today our society should be called on to combat such vices, and the Church should join in this battle. From the Orthodox perspective this is the meaning of the activities for the defence of human rights today.

Chapter 7

HUMAN DIVERSITY AND GLOBAL INTEGRATION

Address to the opening session of the European Council of Religious Leaders, Oslo, 11–12 November 2002

Dear brothers and sisters, dear members of this august gathering! I cordially greet all those present at this first meeting of the European Council of Religious Leaders. I am deeply convinced that it is time to create, on the continent of Europe, an organisation such as this council. The division of Europe into two warring ideological camps now belongs to the past. The twenty-first century does not look set to be the century of ideologies. Too much blood has been shed and too many resources wasted in the twentieth century in the name of ideologies. Humanity is unready, it seems, to repeat this dramatic experience. At the same time it is obvious that ideology has not exhausted its capacity to lead to conflicts and wars.

Contemporary humanity and human culture, in their great diversity, express the beauty and uniqueness of God's creation, and can serve to disclose fully the internal potential He has placed in both individuals and peoples.

There are no two identical peoples, just as there are no two identical individuals. Mankind today includes some of the great civilisational models. These models have much in common, but there are also differences, sometimes very significant. These differences lie not only in the outer forms, but also in values that have emerged under the influence, first of all, of religious factors, but also of the philosophical, political, economic and cultural factors that determine the specificity of a particular civilisational model. Today, for many people, it is obvious that the peaceful future of mankind depends largely on its ability to harmonise the interaction of the existing civilisational models within the context of globalisation.

Talking about the specific features of the Eastern Christian civilisation that arose under the influence of Orthodoxy, we must emphasise the importance for this civilisation of the religious ideal, as it relates not only to the individual, but also to social life and the organisation of family, towns and villages, nation and State. The Christian East also displays other characteristic traits: the unconditional primacy of the spiritual over the material, of self-sacrifice over the desire for worldly success, of the common interest over private concerns, of loyalty to truth and ideals over everyday advantage and earthly well-being.

In Russia, for example, considerable tension is caused in society by attempts to destroy this scale of values under the influence of non-traditional views on personal and public life, advocated primarily by the electronic media and advertising, as well as the growth of consumerism and individualism.

Many of the values inherent in the Eastern Christian civilisation also exist in other civilisational models that have emerged under the decisive influence of the religious factor. Muslim, Jewish and Buddhist worlds have their own traditional systems of values, largely co-terminous with those of Eastern Christianity.

In the Western world, a special civilisational standard would appear to have established itself as the outcome of a philosophical and socio-political development that began during the Renaissance and the Reformation and continued during the Age of Enlightenment and the European revolutions. The basis of this standard is found in the so-called liberal principles which enunciate individual freedom as the highest value. The entire social system is organised in such a way as to make for the fullest possible realisation of individual rights and freedoms.

Since the establishment of international inter-governmental organisations, the axiological system which took shape in the context of Western European and North American social development has formed the basis for the activities of such organisations, and later, the framework for the process of European integration.

It should be noted that the Soviet Union and the then 'Eastern bloc' did not really participate, at a philosophical level, in the development of the foundations of international co-operation. At that time Soviet diplomats pursued different goals, to exploit the system of the UN and other organisations to exercise political and, with it, ideological influence on other states, primarily those of the so-called 'third world'. These diplomats could not, even if they had wanted to, have brought the values of the Eastern Christian tradition into the ideological debate. Such were the circumstances of the time. I am not sure that the diplomats of Muslim countries or of countries with dominant Buddhist cultures were at that time directed by their governments to supplement the ideological basis for international co-operation with the dominant values of the cultures they represented. The historical mistake was the absence at the time of dialogue between politicians and religious leaders who found themselves sidelined from the process of the establishing of inter-governmental organisations. It is important that, at least at the present stage of European integration, with the gradual inclusion of the countries of the former Eastern Europe, some of which belong to the Eastern Christian world and have a significant Muslim and Jewish presence, real dialogue be established and cultivated as far as possible.

This is important because, as mentioned above, it is the values of the Western civilisational model that provide the framework for European integration. So long as European integration is carried out within the boundaries of the Western cultural space, this circumstance is historically justified and sufficiently effective. However, for Europe to become a common home for those who belong to different cultural worlds, the philosophical basis for their integration should include the core values of these worlds. Historical experience clearly demonstrates the fragility of a multicultural, multi-religious society whenever a particular cultural approach is given a monopoly position.

During the Soviet Union, we, Russian believers, had already gathered experience of living in a mono-ideological society. In those days only the Church and cultural worlds were able to create their own space, free from spiritual diktat. And then the totalitarian system, for all its seeming strength and stability, collapsed. This points very strongly to the fundamental unsustainability of a mono-ideological system. Should we not say the same about the current trend towards a monopoly – namely of the Western liberal civilisational standard – despite the existence of other standards followed by millions of people?

This trend is clearly visible, and not only in Europe. It also very obviously dominates the process of globalisation. Equally obvious is the monopoly of a single civilisational standard which is attempting to teach billions of people live to someone else's rules – a truly perilous venture. In an environment where terrorism becomes an instrument of struggle, this dominance can have unpredictable consequences. For certain observers, many of the recent terrorist attacks are an expression of radical opposition to the emerging world order. We even fear a global conflict of civilisations and cultures. Of course, terrorism can never be justified on any account. Mankind must say an emphatic 'no' to any attempts to blackmail and place pressure that result in the death of innocent people. There is also the danger of double standards in the assessment of terrorist activities. People who take hostages and blow up homes in New York or the Middle East should not be qualified as terrorists while those who do the same in Moscow are described as freedom fighters.

We must also do everything possible to ensure that this difference of cultural standards and models is not exploited by those who call for terrorism in the name of a 'holy' struggle for faith and traditional ways of life. The civilisational diversity of the world should lead not to a power confrontation but to co-operation and mutual enrichment. It is important to find a mode of interaction of civilisational models which can ensure a peaceful and prosperous future for the planet.

Of course, no one is calling for the abandonment of the liberal values integrated into the cultures and legal systems of many countries. However, in my view, it is important to supplement these liberal standards with other cultural and philosophical systems, and to create a harmony between the two, not just with declarations of mutual friendship and respect but also through the reform of law and global governance.

We must recognise the equal rights of different cultural and ideological models. Otherwise, a new form of ideological imperialism will provoke even greater conflict than that seen during the colonial era.

We need to ensure that each nation is free to live in harmony with its own choice, with the international system respecting this choice and not trying to impose another. At the international level it is necessary to devise laws and decisions that are equally acceptable to different peoples and to different civilisational models.

The optimal situation here is one in which a liberal standard does not suppress national legislation, but rather promotes a diverse and free development of nations and societies in areas such as State-religion relations, education, culture, and personal, family and community morality. In the event of a conflict for one or another other reason, preference should be given a referendum at national level (in this way society can decide freely on whether to legalise abortion). Before the referendum, all points of view should be represented in the mass media, without traditional attitudes being demeaned or trampled on, or having ideological labels glued to them.

Dear participants of the meeting, never, even in the most tense years of East–West relations, did the idea ever die of restoring European unity in doctrinal, cultural and even political terms. The idea of a united Europe, a comprehensive international union and even a common state in the European space has already existed for more than a thousand years.

But we must understand that the Eastern European countries do not want to follow blindly rules worked out once upon a time in the past by someone without their participation, with no account taken of the vision of their residents, and to follow these rules today simply because they now govern life in materially prosperous Western countries.

Eastern Christian civilisation, as any other, has created its own distinctive way of life. Its philosophy and its general format reflect the efforts of many generations of professing Orthodoxy people who have striven to build a personal and public life that reflects their religious and cultural traditions.

I am deeply convinced that the present social system needs to enable people to live and act according to the norms of their faith. For this reason it is wrong to limit the participation of the Church and other religions only to the discussion of issues relating to the problems of their legal status, inter-faith relations and the like. I bear witness that the representatives of our Church are ready to participate in the discussion of issues of European security, social work, ethics of the use of modern technologies, etc. A key task in our co-operation with European and international institutions should be the creation of a multi-format mechanism for dialogue among civilisations.

Among the specific initiatives concerning the participation of religious leaders in the life of modern Europe I would mention the need for our Council to engage in systematic dialogue with the European Parliament, the European Commission, the Council of Europe, and other European and international structures. We should think about practical arrangements for such interaction, possibly in the form of establishing a permanent representative office of the European Council of Religious Leaders to the European Institutions.

Religious leaders have something to say to politicians. We are also willing to listen to them – to listen to in order to understand how we can best serve mankind and promote the peace and unity of the human family. I very much hope that our dialogue with the European structures of governance will become permanent and systematic, open and serious, to the benefit of the people of our continent.

Chapter 8

THE RUSSIAN ORTHODOX CHURCH AND THE CHRISTIAN DIMENSION OF THE PROBLEM OF HUMAN RIGHTS AND FREEDOMS

Article published in the newspaper Izvestia, *4 April 2006*

The single biggest issue for our contemporary world is the relation-ship of the concept of the rights and freedoms of the individual with the question of moral responsibility. Christian thought characteristi-cally links the idea of human dignity with the question of morality, which inevitably leads us to reflect on the devastating effect of sin on the soul. Liberal philosophy, on the other hand, which ignores the concept of sin, lacks the distinction between good and bad which religion makes. For me, it is this absence that explains the inherent inconsistency of the modern Western world's understanding of human rights.

Ousting the concept of sin from everyday life and from the sphere of intellectual discourse leads to a blurring of the borderline between good and evil in peoples' consciousness. The only thing that is forbidden is for people to realise themselves in a manner that could restrict another person's freedom. In other words, the law of the land must be respected, but moral imperatives are totally unnecessary. Which is why religious ethics, which insists on the primacy of moral values, is today under violent attack. It is declared obsolete, an obstacle to progress. At best it is tolerated, providing it does not contradict the basic tenets of liberalism.

All this adds up to a fundamental contradiction between the religious and secular approaches to the theme of human dignity. The Russian Orthodox Church was the first to formulate this problem, which cannot be swept under the carpet, and bring it into the international arena.

Why has the debate about human dignity and human rights became so topical? Primarily because the Orthodox world is gradually becoming part of the common European space. Many Orthodox states have entered or are about to enter the European Union. And even if Russia's integration into the EU is still a long way off, we already find ourselves today a part of a common European space. This certainly applies in the sphere of law, with the legislative process in the Russian Federation largely aligned on existing Western European legal standards.

Whether we like it not, Russia belongs to the pan-European space culturally, geographically, historically, politically and psychologically. But even so, in the current process of integration we should not accept uncritically, like slaves, liberal behaviours and values formed without our direct involvement. Russia, with its thousand-year spiritual, cultural, theological and intellectual tradition, should not uncritically adopt the ideas that have emerged in the context of Western culture, just as it should not reject them simply because they have been developed outside Russia.

Unfortunately, our sincere desire to analyse impartially and to interpret this complex of ideas is frequently rejected out of hand. Moreover, any independent, critical attitude towards secular liberalism, which now serves as an ideological support of integration processes in the new Europe, inevitably attracts hostility. Today, moreover, we unfortunately observe the appearance of symptoms indicating a desire in some liberal circles to use force to combat traditionalism, including religious practices and values.

As we know, the United States has in recent years experienced a vigorous offensive of secularist ideology. For example, in California it is forbidden to set up Christmas trees in public, a prohibition all the more amazing when we learn that in Israel, where Judaism is the state religion, these symbols of Christmas are distributed free of charge to

Christians under a special government programme. The French law
prohibiting the public wearing of prominent public religious symbols
has provoked fierce public debate on the issue of inalienable rights,
including the freedom of religion. Recently, the European media
focused on the story of how one of Europe's intellectuals was
deprived of a top position in the European Commission simply for
speaking on the issue of homosexuality in the spirit of the Christian
tradition. Then there was the scandalous case of a Swedish Pentecos-
talist pastor being sent to prison for calling sodomy a sin in a sermon.
Both Europe and Russia have already lived through dramatic and
unforgettable periods of different social classes or social groupings
defending their ideas by force and depriving others of the right to
express their beliefs. In such cases, the triumph of the ideology of the
former has ultimately always required if not the physical, then at least
the moral destruction of dissidents. For us, it is clear that the principle
of priority of individual rights and freedoms in the context of
international relations should be based on a broad consensus of all
interested parties and not on an arbitrary and selective interpretation
of this principle, and *a fortiori*, not serve any one particular political or
ideological order.

For me, the fundamental problem is summed up in the following
question: how in the proposed community of peoples can the new
world order be consistent with religious principles? In my view, it is
wrong and even dangerous when people attempt to embrace the
entire vast variety of God's world with a small number of ideas
formulated in the Western European philosophical and political
context, without the meaningful participation of Muslims, Jews,
Buddhists, Hindus and Orthodox Christians, and of Catholics as
well. Indeed, the large majority of the world's population, with their
ancient and native cultures, has never participated meaningfully in
the development of this value system, which people want to set up as
a universal standard, at times even by force.

There is a danger that those who are unable to respond adequately
to this pressure may well opt for resistance by force. It is not hard to
push religious people to the act of self-sacrifice, to find meaning to
their lives in defending what is sacred for them. Nor should we

exclude the possibility of malicious people exploiting this latent, but real, resistance of believers to the impending wave of aggressive liberalism in order to incite violence, as is already the case with the Islamic resistance to the 'law on wearing head scarves' or to blasphemous depictions of the prophet Muhammad.

On the other hand, it is clear that the globalisation process must sooner or later lead us to agree on common fundamental values. Otherwise it will not be possible to coexist constructively in a single civilisational space.

But at the same time, in my opinion, there is a need for further discussion on how secular liberal values, in the form in which they exist today, can lay claim to be universal, and as to whether these values can, without a corresponding correction, form the basis for the formation of new relationships between people, countries and peoples in our era of globalisation.

This situation clearly demonstrates the vital importance in the modern world of inter-civilisational dialogue and the harmonisation of different cultural and historical models in the interest of all mankind. This is no easy task today, but this pressing problem is becoming one of the priorities facing the global community.

Chapter 9

GIVING A SOUL TO EUROPE

Opening address to an international conference, 'Giving a Soul to Europe – Mission and Responsibility of the Church', organised jointly by the Department of Foreign Church Relations of the Moscow Patriarchate and the Papal Commission for Culture, Vienna, 3–5 May 2006

Today we have gathered to discuss a common concern, the focal point for which is Europe. Europe: a unique cultural and spiritual phenomenon that has been shaped over the centuries and is currently undergoing fundamental changes. Why should we, as representatives of the Russian Orthodox Church, be concerned at the fate of Europe? Because Russia, while possessing its own distinctive culture and self-consciousness, is also an integral part of Europe. It is not by chance that Dostoevsky, who like nobody else was conscious of Russia's uniqueness, nevertheless called Europe his second home. In the Russian soul, Europe occupies a special place, primarily because of its Christian roots. I would like to stress that these roots go back not only to Western Christianity, but also to Eastern Christianity, mainly through Byzantium.

Historians tell us that the very name Byzantium is artificial and came into use only in the sixteenth century in the West. Until then, Byzantium was known as the Roman or Romaian empire, and the Byzantines called themselves Romans or Romaians. From its capital of Constantinople, this empire extended both westwards and eastwards. With its eastern and western parts it decisively influenced the formation of modern European civilisation. For example, nobody will contest the assertion that St Augustine is a father of Western European thought, but it should be remembered that Eastern neo-

Platonists exerted decisive influence on him. Western Scholasticism, which became the cradle of modern philosophy, was formed under the influence of the Eastern Cappadocians and the Corpus Areopagiticum. The legal culture of Western Europe grew out of the Code of Civil Law of Emperor Justinian. And even after the tragic division of Western and Eastern Christendom, the Byzantines continued to exert tremendous influence on Western thought and culture. It is not by chance that the mass emigration of educated Greeks to Italy after the capture of Constantinople by the Turks in the fifteenth century coincided with the beginning of the Italian Renaissance. Vestiges of Byzantine culture in the West can be seen even today in the Cathedral of St Mark in Venice and in the Spanish paintings of the Cretan iconographer Domenikos Theotokopoulos, known as El Greco.

In modern times, great Russian writers, artists and composers inspired by the Orthodox spiritual tradition have made their unique contribution to the formation of Western European literature, painting and music. One could cite innumerable examples of such influences and the intertwining of West and East in Europe's history. All this leads us to state that Europe's identity has been formed under the influence of both Western and Eastern culture, and of both Western and Eastern Christianity. For the reasons just indicated, the processes taking place now in what I would not hesitate to call our common European home cannot but concern Russia and also the Russian Orthodox Church, whose canonical territory extends far beyond Russia's boundaries and into the West.

What is occurring in modern Europe? We are all observers of a dramatic weakening that is taking place in Europe's Christian identity. Europe is losing the characteristics given to it by Christianity, both Western and Eastern Christianity alike. Borrowing some words from the title of our conference, Europe is losing its soul. Over the centuries the Christian soul of Europe gave it life, made it remarkably attractive for the most remote countries and peoples and endowed its culture with universal character.

European values are becoming more and more secular, but I would not say that these values have totally lost their ties with Christianity. Many of them could never have appeared if there had been no

Christianity in Europe. They represent a watered-down, worldly version of traditional European Christian values. And it is this devitalised version that is often turned against the Christianity that gave birth to these values, casting doubt on the Christian identity of Europe. Breaking with the spiritual foundations of European civilisation, these values risk losing the good that was placed in them by Christianity. Our concern is that Europe, having lost its connection to Christianity, may end up exercising forms of oppression or even violence against the individual that have always been foreign to her. Russia, as no other country, has experienced just how grave the break with one's spiritual roots can be for civilisation, something that threatens societies not only with the loss of their countenance, but also with the rise of violence toward the person, flagrant violations of personal freedom and a brutal disregard for people's spiritual needs. The history of Russia in the twentieth century can act as a warning to Western Europe: the rejection of the spiritual and cultural bases of one or the other civilisation can represent a serious threat to civilisation itself. Indeed, the forms of social relations that were shaped in twentieth century Russia were to a significant extent secularised variants of values characteristic of the Russian spiritual tradition: collectivism was a secularised variant of *sobornost* and the communal idea, a single-state ideology, substituted the spiritual authority of the Church, and so on and so forth. The effects of this substitution are well-known to everyone. For this reason, secularism, the break with spiritual traditions, represents such a great threat to the existence of European civilisation.

Today one can point to the dramatic rise in Europe's Muslim population. In view of this, can Europe remain Christian while not entering into conflict with Islam? The recent scandal caused by the publication of caricatures of the prophet Muhammad demonstrates that it is not Christianity that causes collisions, but rather secularism – the secularisation of society – which behaves with disdain toward spiritual values and the sacred. In this regard, the positive example of Russia – where Orthodoxy, Islam and other traditional religions peacefully coexist to the extent that respect for faith and sacred things is maintained in society – is remarkable. In other words, Islam is ready to coexist peacefully with Christianity. Extremism, rooted in radical sentiments within Islam, is as a rule directed not against Christianity itself but against the lack of spirituality and the secularisation of Western societies. Of course, we do not attempt to justify extremism, but simply speak of the causes that give rise to it. Thus, the secularisation of Europe not only undermines the foundations of European identity but also provokes conflict with religious groups which do not wish to subject themselves to the general tendency of secularisation.

In view of this, it seems to me extremely important to return to the Christian meaning of the European values that underwent secularisation, central to which are freedom and human rights. In their secularised form these values, as mentioned above, lose their profundity and can even turn against the person and the spiritual foundations of his personality. A month ago, from 4–6 April 2006, the Tenth World Russian People's Council was held in Moscow. One of the highlights of this forum was the adoption of the Declaration on the Rights and Dignity of the Person. Some have already christened this document a specifically Russian declaration of human rights, affirming an understanding of rights opposite to the Western understanding. Such was not, however, the task of those who prepared this declaration. Their task was rather to give a Christian interpretation of certain fundamental categories – those of human rights and liberties – that drive world politics today. We have attempted to integrate a theological foundation into this concept of human rights, thereby uniting, or rather re-uniting, this concept with traditional Christian views. We have attempted to demonstrate the Christian roots of the human rights concept.

This declaration makes a fundamental distinction between two meanings of human dignity, which we have agreed to call value and dignity, as well as between two meanings of freedom: freedom as the non-determinate nature of human actions, and freedom as not being subjugated to evil and sin. The fact that man is created in the image of God, as well as the fact of the Incarnation, that is the assumption by the Son of God of our nature for the salvation of the human race, serve as the basis for the affirmation of the pre-eminent value of human nature. This value cannot be taken away or destroyed by other people, society, the State, etc. An integral part of human nature that gives it special value is the freedom of choice. This freedom was placed into human nature by God Himself and cannot be violated by anyone: not other people, not evil forces, not even God himself.

By itself, this freedom is only an instrument with which the person realises his moral choices. Freedom of choice should be used for attaining freedom from sin. Only by liberating oneself from the shackles of sin and acquiring the 'freedom of the glory of God's children', as St Paul wrote in his Epistle to the Romans (8:21), can a person give meaning to his inherent ability to make free choices and acquire that which in the Declaration is called dignity. Human dignity is the highest goal of existence. Expressed in theological terms, it corresponds to the likeness of God in the person. Dignity is acquired when one makes his choices in favour of the good, and is lost when one chooses evil.

Just as freedom of choice, human rights, to which the Declaration is dedicated, are instruments that should serve the higher goal of the moral perfection of the person. On the one hand, the Declaration recognises human rights as an important social establishment that defends people as God's creation from infringements from outside. On the other hand, it places the category of human rights into a moral context. The text of the Declaration states: 'We are for the right to life and against the "right" to death, for the right to creation and against the "right" to destruction. We acknowledge the rights and liberties of the person to the extent that they help the person rise toward the good, protect him from internal and external evil, and help him to realise his potential positively in society.'

Therefore, as mentioned in the text of the Declaration: 'Rights and liberties are inextricably connected with the obligations and responsibilities of the person.' In the Declaration, the categories of the liberties and rights of the person received an additional, very important dimension – the moral dimension. This dimension sets a higher goal to the essentially instrumental categories of the freedom of choice and rights. Thanks to this moral dimension, the category of human rights acquires a teleological completion and a goal that lies beyond its own boundaries, in the realm of the most profound areas of human existence. From this perspective, the Declaration contains a more multi-faceted, complex and holistic approach to the problem of human rights, an approach that reflects the fact that the person bears the image of God and that his existence should have moral significance.

Along with the participants of the Tenth World Russian People's Council, we too can testify to the fact that the welfare and perhaps the very existence of human civilisation in a globalised world will to a great extent depend on the ability to combine rights and freedoms with moral responsibility. For this, the freedom and morality that have been placed by God Himself into human nature, and which belong to everyone regardless of their culture or religion, are able to unite the existing civilisational models in a peaceful and viable manner.

Chapter 10

HUMAN RIGHTS AND THEIR MORAL FOUNDATIONS IN EUROPEAN RELIGIOUS COMMUNITIES

Presentation at the seminar 'Evolution of Moral Values and Human Rights in Multicultural Society', Strasbourg, 30 October 2006

First of all, let me say how much I appreciate the opportunity to speak about the Russian Orthodox Church's view on human rights precisely here in Strasbourg, at a forum made available by the Council of Europe. There are two reasons for this satisfaction. The first is that it is in an 'experienced' organisation, which for a number of decades has accumulated great knowledge in and means of handling this realm, that I present the Orthodox vision of human rights. The second is the value I attach to the fact of this conference is taking place. It speaks of how the Council of Europe is open to listening to the voices of various cultures in the European area. For me, this testifies to the fact that the Council of Europe is not an elite club remote from society, but a vital channel of communication between the peoples of Europe, which includes the subject of the values by which they live.

Last April, the Holy Synod of the Russian Orthodox Church took a decision to produce a document reflecting its view on human rights and the advocacy of the same. The development of this document has only just begun. Therefore I can only point here to the directions which this work is taking and how it poses the problem. As we are aware, the results of any work are greatly influenced by the motives behind it. Therefore, to begin with, I would like to outline two fundamental reasons for which the Russian Orthodox Church today raises the question of human rights.

First of all, now is the most suitable time for profound reflection upon this conception from the position of our thousand-year spiritual and national tradition. It is no secret that the concept of human rights and its institutions are an idea and reality which have taken shape in Western culture. Therefore their borrowing requires adaptation to the concrete life of a particular people. Unfortunately, after the Second World War, when the topic of human rights became ever more relevant in international relations and occupied a leading position in the internal life of many countries, the Russian Orthodox Church was deprived of the opportunity to discuss this topic freely. In Soviet society human rights were not regarded as a serious challenge. In signing international agreements in defence of human rights, the Soviet Union had in mind its own standards of human rights, the inviolability of which were upheld by the power of the State. Today, no external forces put the Russian Orthodox Church under pressure; therefore it is able to express freely its opinion of human rights. Moreover, these considerations are based on my own small yet practical experience of fifteen years of living in societies based on human rights norms.

The second reason is that the Russian Orthodox Church is endeavouring to contribute to making human rights something genuinely universal. I have often chanced to hear the view that Russians want to come up with their own notion of human rights, convenient to them, and then justify it by any means possible. I would like to make it clear that nobody has ever invented a means of speaking of universal norms other than in the language of their own national culture. To this day, the understanding and application of human rights bear the serious cultural imprint of the West. This is perhaps not so noticeable in the West, yet it is obvious in the East, in Asia, Latin America and Africa. It is therefore too early to say that a universal vision of human rights exists. Indeed, we are only on the verge of hammering out a truly universal understanding of human rights to which each culture will make its contribution. I believe this to be one of the priority tasks of dialogue between civilisations.

I do not deny that the West has made and continues to make a very weighty and significant contribution to this process. Yet it is essential to listen to other voices. In turning to the language of its national culture, each nation turns towards that which is universal within it. Russian culture is especially sensitive to the universal concerns of the human person. It contains a tradition of reflecting upon the topics of freedom, mercy and philanthropy. This is witnessed by Russian theology, spirituality, philosophy, literature and art, which have been studied with interest in other countries. These are the motives which underlie the work of the Russian Church on the topic of human rights.

Now allow me to present those basic lines along which the working group responsible for preparing the document on human rights is thinking. We believe that this document ought to begin by reflecting upon the ideological nucleus of human rights and then come to some practical conclusions. It is obvious that the central idea of the concept of human rights is the notion of the value of the human person. In accordance with this view the well-being of each person ought to constitute the main goal of any social order. I would say that this view is a result of humanity's suffering in the terrible wars of the twentieth century, which were instigated under the influence of the idea of national, racial, ideological or economic supremacy. Humanity has seen that this is a dead end. It leads nowhere. Each life and each person has value and is called to a good life. And this idea, which is embedded in human rights, finds a response in the hearts of many people throughout the globe, independent of their faith and nationality.

Of course, Christianity cannot but respond to this idea, as it was precisely Christianity which nourished it. How can it be otherwise if, in the eyes of God who created the world, the human person occupies a special place and enjoys His special love? In the Bible God's relation to man is expressed by the Greek word *agape* – love. In the tradition of Christian thought this love is made real and is transformed into the concrete notion of love of humanity. The holy fathers call God the lover of humanity. In Orthodox worship this definition of God is the one that is encountered most often of all.

Each person is called upon to embody this very principle in his relations with his neighbour. If the person does not act in this way, he goes against God. For its part, the Russian theological, philosophical and literary tradition has always accorded and continues to accord priority to the theme of the human person and love of the person. Quite recently the famous writer Alexander Solzhenitsyn once more expressed this idea in relation to the practical sphere, saying that 'the care and well-being of the people is the most important of all the tasks of the State'.

However, love for the human person signifies a certain under-standing of his well-being which is based upon the notion of the human person. Also important is the means by which this well-being is attained. It is quite possible to humiliate someone and believe that we are doing him good. Therefore the goal and means need to accord with each other in the single spirit of love for humanity. In modern multicultural society there exists a remarkable unanimity regarding the well-being of the human person. However, it touches upon only the material aspect of human life. Of course, there is nothing wrong with this, as our love of neighbour ought to signify concern for his material well-being also. It is therefore perfectly right that the State should strive to build an effective economy and create a system of social security for the human person.

At the same time (and unfortunately this has to be said) concern for the spiritual welfare of the human person is left today to the discretion of the individual and is not an object of concern for State and society. At first glance the notion that each defines for himself what serves his spiritual well-being sounds very agreeable and elevated. But in fact it turns out that in withdrawing from this sphere, the State and society lease out the topic of morality in the public sphere to interest groups who attain power, make money and gratify their personal ambitions on the spiritual vices of the human person. This situation is justified as being the free choice of those people who consume this product. However, it is not difficult to create a demand for amoral products if we bear in mind the very unstable moral condition of human nature. There is an ancient Christian story in which a hermit came with his young disciple to a large town to buy certain necessities. They were met by a prostitute who said to the hermit: 'You have laboured for many years with this young man in order to educate him in virtue. Would you like me to destroy your labours in a single minute?' The hermit replied that he quite willingly believed her, as it was far more difficult to climb a mountain than descend from it.

This is an extraordinary thing: we know how to act properly and how we ought to live, yet the false attraction of vice and our weak-willedness draw us in the opposite direction. Humanity has known this truth since time immemorial. In his Epistle to the Romans, St Paul expressed this laconically: 'I do not do what I want, but I do the very thing I hate' (Rom. 7:15). The cause of this human condition is sin, which distorts human nature. It is uncustomary to speak of sin in the modern world. The secular world has simply made this word taboo. At the same time, for many religions this word is one of the key words in understanding the state of human nature. The non-religious person knows from everyday life that we are capable of mistakes and incorrect actions that do harm to ourselves and others. Thus, sin is a universal concept. However, from this concept we need to derive the correct conclusion. Society should not punish people for breach of morality, if in their personal life they do not live according to moral statutes. Yet in public life society ought to uphold moral directions since the human person needs this support because of his moral weakness. What is now happening in our countries goes completely against this task. In the public realm, especially in the mass media, one is not called upon to observe moral standards but, rather, various means are used to convince one of the necessity of transgressing them. As a result, society deprives people of the freedom of moral development and perfection.

The withdrawal of society and the State from supporting traditional moral norms has resulted in society confronting situations in which the religious feelings of major groups are offended, or in which pseudo-religious movements are allowed to use the public arena to advertise and propagate their views. Moreover, in both national and international law, standards which contradict traditional morality are being introduced and form part of government policy.

We arrive at a situation in which the minority imposes its standards upon the majority. In Europe it has become a commonplace, for everything that is connected to Christianity is removed from the public realm in order not to offend the feelings of representatives of other religions. That results in connivance at the intolerance of religious minorities and the diminishing of the rights of the religious majority. What do people see? The inability of human rights to defend their cultural and religious traditions. It is at this stage that they join the ranks of the extreme right, and we are surprised why these political tendencies find support at the ballot box.

I am convinced that the concern for spiritual needs, based moreover on traditional morality, ought to return to the public realm. The upholding of moral standards must become a social cause. It is the mechanism of human rights that can actively enable this return. I talk about returning, because this standard of the harmonisation of human rights and traditional morality is contained in the Universal Declaration of Human Rights of 1948. In particular, it states: 'In the exercise of his rights and freedoms, everyone shall be subject only to such limitations as are determined by law solely for the purpose of securing due recognition and respect for the rights and freedoms of others and of meeting the just requirements of morality, public order and the general welfare in a democratic society' (Article 29.2).

The topic of morality proceeds from the question of the purpose and meaning of the institution of human rights. Freedom cannot be an end in itself; otherwise, we will be forced to admit its extreme manifestations too, which lead to the self-destruction of the human person and the collapse of society. For example, the problem of giving offence to religious feelings consists not of whether freedom of speech or freedom of creative work should exist, but of how this freedom is used. The tragedy of modern-day human rights advocates is that they do not sense that an individual or a group of people can use freedom not for the good, but to the detriment of others in pursuing their narrow interests.

However, the understanding of what is good and what is bad will not be made manifest by itself. Rousseau's optimistic view of human nature has long since been shown to be utopian. It is my profound conviction that the principle of freedom, which is today defended by human rights institutions, ought to be harmonised with morality and faith. This harmonisation ought to be reflected in the structure of contemporary society. In the opposite instance a social system built exclusively upon human rights will be fragile and self-destructive.

One of the arguments against the presence of moral standards in the public realm is the assertion that there is no single morality. The opponents of upholding morality in public life say that there are as many opinions as there are people, which means as many approaches to morality. No, there is a single morality. Within the confines of the Ten Commandments, the major world religions agree among themselves. It is also with these commandments that, as a rule, secular ethics also agree. The unity of morality is based upon the human characteristic of conscience. Various philosophical traditions may ascribe this to various sources. Christianity states that it is a divine law inscribed within the human person, suggesting to him what is dangerous for him and what is not.

This was once more affirmed by the various meetings in which the Russian Orthodox Church has actively participated this year. The topic of human rights was discussed by representatives of Russian society and people of Russian culture from various countries at the World Russian Peoples' Council. There were discussions between the Russian Orthodox Church and the Roman Catholic Church in Vienna last May. Moscow hosted a summit of religious leaders at the beginning of July. In September, together with the Council of Europe, Nizhny Novgorod hosted the 'Dialogue of Cultures and Inter-Religious Co-operation' conference. All of these meetings showed that not only between the various Christian confessions is there a common understanding of moral standards, but also between the main world religious communities and even secular moral value systems. At all conferences we found a pretty wide platform that is shared by each religious or secular force. Of course, we believe in God in different ways, yet we relate to peoples' religious feelings in identical ways, and we do not believe that it is permissible to offend them for the sake of freedom of expression.

Why is the opinion of the majority ignored and not taken into account in the structure of modern-day society? It is this question which we address today to the world community. We understand that harmonising freedom of personal moral choice with the moral values of society is an extremely difficult task. It will not be resolved by interdictions and controls alone. Education in moral behaviour ought to be a social aim. No political or economic interests ought to distort this goal. However, the human person should have the freedom of choice in his personal life; in other words, he should have the opportunity not to adhere to norms. In this instance, neither the State nor society should implement any sanctions or penalties. Yet from the television screen one ought not to be taught how to find a mistress but how to set up and keep together a family, not how to earn a living dishonestly but how to do so by honest labour.

For the moral norms and values of religious traditions to be present in the public domain, it is essential to set up mechanisms of dialogue between the structures of the authorities and religious communities, and of interaction between society and religion. Religious organisations ought to have the chance to enter into dialogue and have a genuine influence upon fundamental decision-making, since they are the main bearers of moral values in any society. It is essential to have a multilateral dialogue both at the national and international levels. It would be good if the Council of Europe, the European Union and United Nations were to develop consultative organs which would enter into dialogue with religious organisations.

In today's conditions of the multiculturalism of practically every society, no one religion can lay claim to special status. However, the place of each religion in society and its contribution to the life of society must be considered. The political and social system ought to be constructed so that religious organisations can work with their followers, including the social sphere: in the fields of education, health care, social service and so on. Therefore, in those countries where the Russian Church has a presence it speaks out for the teaching of Orthodox culture in secular schools, for the introduction of chaplaincies, the presence of religious topics in the media and the social ministry of religious organisations. Today, Orthodox public opinion is seeking to be included in the advocacy of human rights in all realms of social life. In this way there are plans to set up a human rights centre under the World Russian Peoples' Council. I am convinced that the experience that we will gain here will help us to reflect upon the meaning of defending human rights. I would like to emphasise that in this process we are open to dialogue and co-operation with all forces in society.

Chapter 11

THE VALUE OF THE HUMAN BEING AS THE BEARER OF THE IMAGE OF GOD AND HIS DIGNITY

Address to the seminar 'Loyalty to Traditional Christian Values and Freedom of Conscience', Moscow, 20 December 2006

The great Russian classical writer, Anton Chekhov, once said, through the mouth of the hero of his well-known play, *Uncle Vanya*: 'Everything in man should be beautiful: his face, his clothing, his soul, his mind.' If in the play the hero (the doctor, Michael Levovich Astrov) utters it more sneeringly than seriously, this phrase has nevertheless become widely quoted. By using the word 'should', the writer has enunciated a sort of general rule. This tells us that in most people lies a deep-seated desire for improvement, a dissatisfaction with the present state of man and the desire to correct it.

Dissatisfaction with man's current situation and the desire to improve it are common to any culture and to most religious traditions which have a high idea of man's destiny.

At the same time, most peoples of the world understand that there is something in human nature or in the outside world that prevents man from fulfilling that purpose. Put simply, universal experience tells us that naïve and empty self-satisfaction at man's present condition, and the blind defence of everything that is in man at a given moment, cannot serve as a serious basis to humanity.

Different religious and philosophical traditions offer their various ways of bridging this gap in man's inner world. Christianity most clearly captures this ambivalent position of man and offers the most direct way to overcome it: what, in Christian language, is called salvation.

The biblical story of the Creation tells unambiguously of the high position that man originally occupied in the created world. Man crowned the earthly creation as it appeared at the end of God's creative act. Indeed God created man in a very special way, by breathing His own breath into already created matter. Whereupon God created a special home for man on earth, the Garden of Eden, giving him dominion over all living creatures.

The great fourth-century theologian, St Gregory Nazianzen, writes of man's place in the created world: 'The life-creating Word creates a living being in the form of man that shows the unity of both invisible and visible nature. From already created matter he takes the body, but from Himself inserts life, to create a sort of second world, a macrocosm within a microcosm. He places on earth another angel, a worshipper drawn from different races, a spectator of visible creation, holder of the secret of contemplatable creation, king over everything on earth, subject of the heavenly kingdom' (*Second Sermon for Easter*, ch. 6–7).

Peculiar to human nature, in the common Christian view, are the image and likeness of God, placed in it by God at Creation and inseparable from it. Commonly, no distinction is made between these two words of Sacred Scripture – image and likeness – which are considered as denoting the same thing. Nevertheless, the very use of two expressions is not accidental, because behind them lie two different aspects of the involvement of human nature in the life of the Deity.

Another great Christian theologian, St Basil the Great, very clearly explains the difference between the two: 'We receive the one by our creation, we acquire the other of our free will. In the initial dispensation it was given to us to be born in God's image, through our free will is formed in us being the likeness of God ... "Let us make man in our image" (Gen. 1:26). Man has command over creation according in the image, but he is also intended to become in accordance with the likeness. God gave him the power to do so. If He had created you in the likeness also, what would you stand to gain? Why would you be crowned? And if the Creator gave you everything, simply opened up the kingdom of heaven for you? But the fact is that one part is given to you, but the other part remains incomplete. This is so that man can complete this other part himself, and be worthy of the reward coming from God' (*On the Origin of Man*, I, 16–17).

Although based on human values, the contemporary political and legal systems of all civilised countries fail to reflect this dynamic nature of the human person. State and society are very often called upon to defend man as he is. Of course, there is nothing wrong with a situation in which people are accepted and defended regardless of religion, nationality, gender or age. But increasingly, State and society are ceasing to assist the spiritual development of man towards any, even the most elementary of, moral goals. This non–intervention they justify by the duty of protection of personal freedom of choice and the reluctance to push people to do anything.

In my opinion, this disengagement of State and society from people's moral and spiritual education does not reflect the natural needs of each person, and is therefore doomed to dire consequences. The social structure must reflect and support man's aspiration to improve, otherwise it will deteriorate and fall apart.

Of course, in today's multi–religious society, both within the borders of the individual state and on a global scale, it is impossible to apply Christian theological concepts as a foundation for this property of human nature. The concept of 'human dignity', properly under-stood, might well help in addressing this problem. In its first sense, 'dignity' refers to a certain position which a person takes in a particular system: of the universe, or of one or the other social or political structure. In addition, we use the word 'dignity' to assert positively the value of man. Of a villain we never say that he has dignity, because his actions do not correspond to man's high destiny. This concept of dignity can be correlated with the biblical notion of the likeness. At the same time, the biblical concept of the image is very close to the concept of the inherent value of man. Indeed, Christians believe that the image of God is indelible from man. It can be darkened, but not removed. For this reason any and every person has value, regardless of his actions and the state of mind.

In my opinion, today we must not just talk on every corner of the dignity of man, but do everything possible to contribute to its development. Dignity is not something granted. It is something that must be fought for and nurtured. This does not mean that I propose to conduct a selection exercise and determine who has this dignity, and who does not. We simply should not consider as dignity that which already exists in every person. This is a fallacy and an error.

Dignity is something that has to be developed. I believe it is the duty of the State and society to confront each person with the task of developing his or her dignity. They not only have to guarantee people's freedom, but also to try to give it some sort of direction, by introducing and promoting examples of good living.

I am confident that such a dynamic understanding of human dignity would help us build a system of social development which would more adequately answer to the needs of human nature.

Chapter 12

INTER-CIVILISATIONAL DIALOGUE

Address to the seminar, 'Dialogue between Cultures and Civilisations: a Bridge between Human Rights and Moral Values', Paris, 13–14 March 2007

Let me start by thanking the organisers for gathering in Paris representatives of various religious communities and political and social institutions to discuss the pressing and topical issue of human rights. I especially value the opportunity to speak today within the walls of a renowned international organisation, representing the UN system and concerning itself with science, education and culture in the world. Given UNESCO's specific sphere of competence, I would like to consider the proposed topic in a cultural perspective. As you well know, culture can be interpreted both in a narrow and in a broad sense. In the narrow sense of the word, culture refers to certain forms of expression, based on the aesthetic sense inherent in human nature. In a broad sense, culture is the whole complex of values that guide the life of the individual and society. Consequently, culture has a significant influence on political, social and economic life.

Today, many stable cultural systems exist, based on different religions and different historical experiences. In such a diverse world there is, of course, a problem of mutual understanding between cultures, the differences between which can lead not only to co-operation but also to conflict.

However, the risk of conflict derives not only from the relations between distinct cultures, each with its own geographical area. In the context of globalisation, we are inevitably seeing take shape a global culture that is common to all peoples of the world, and which international organisations have taken upon themselves to define and police. The proper role of such a global culture should, however, be to serve as a bridge between different civilisations, not to seek to subordinate them to its standards. In recent years, however, we have seen the contrary: increasing tension between so-called universal values and cultural identities.

Today, human rights are recognised as such universal values. From the outset, human rights have been emphatically shaped as a secular value, understandable by and acceptable to all people, regardless of ideological position. In turn, the secular nature of this concept serves as a basis for certain forces to assert that it is not open to influence by religion, and that religion itself should submit to its rules. I can confidently say that many religious traditions of the world today do not question the fact that the language of human rights must remain a secular language. At least the Orthodox tradition does not. But on the body of human rights and their realisation, the religious world has every right to bring its influence to bear, as does any other ideology. And when I talk of the body of human rights, I have in mind a set of specific rights and freedoms. It is known that the list of such rights was formed gradually, beginning with civil and political rights, and is still in the process of formation.

The body of rights and freedoms should not be dogmatic in character. If we repeat the mistake of the Marxists and dogmatise socio-political doctrines, labelling all who dissent from them as revisionists, this will not bring about mutual understanding in society. The doctrine of human rights originated in Western Europe in specific historical conditions, and can and should evolve with the changing world. Of particular importance here is the use people make of their human rights. For example, a person given the freedom to possess a firearm for self-defence is also at liberty to break into a school and shoot his classmates. In other words, human rights provide opportunities, but their use depends on a person's ideological position towards right and wrong.

After asserting that religious organisations are entitled to bring their influence to bear on both the content and the realisation of human rights, I would like to clarify the direction in which, and the means by which, they seek to do so. Last year, the theme of human rights was widely discussed in Russian society. Today, Russia is facing many challenges, and is now rethinking much of what previously seemed obvious. In April last year the Tenth World Russian People's Council held in Moscow focused on the theme of human rights. In passing I would point out that the World Russian People's Council is an international organisation that has consultative status with ECOSOC. This council serves as a platform to discuss current issues of social development from the viewpoint of the originality of Russian culture. This annual event gathers representatives of traditional religions, governments and society in Russia, and from Russian communities around the world. The Council is headed by the Patriarch of Moscow and All Russia, Alexy II. The debate which began at the Council then spilled over into Russian society at large and is still very much alive.

One starting point of the Russian Orthodox Church's reasoning on human rights is the freedom of the individual. So today, when someone says that the Russian Church, which initiated a debate on human rights, is trying to eliminate human rights or to invent some new interpretation of them, this is simply not true. Freedom is inalienable because it is part of human nature created by God. If the Russian Church were to preach anything else, this would be contrary to the divine teachings. However, our church, as well as the social forces which support it, asserts the need to reconcile human rights with the support of traditional moral values in society. Which begs the question: what are these values? And how do they appear in society – are they contractual in nature or do these values have a universal character? The World Russian People's Council responded to these questions, stating in its declaration that there are moral values that are supported by an absolute majority of the religious traditions of the world, as well as secular schools of thought.

To check its findings with other peoples and religious traditions of the world, the Russian Church has held a series of consultations over the past year. Last May, in conversations with the Roman Catholic Church, we found that our churches have the same vision on many issues. In July, Moscow hosted the summit of religious leaders, which was attended by representatives of many of the world's traditional religions from 49 countries. The Council of Europe has also expressed interest in the debate raised by the Russian Church. Under its aegis, conferences took place in Nizhny Novgorod and Strasbourg. We found that most religious traditions of the world and some secular currents of thought coincide in their definition of the contours of moral values. And what should we do when there are people who disagree with the traditional morality that is shared by most people in the world? After all, democracy is particularly sensitive to the non-discrimination against people of different views in society. How do we organise society in such a way that the majority lives in accordance with its values, but the minority is not discriminated against? These questions led us to consider how the Moscow Patriarchate sees the mechanics of how religion influences the the formation of international and national norms and values.

Unfortunately, the development of contemporary international law often follows the path of imposing the views of various minorities onto the majority of the planet. And in this we see a dangerous trend that threatens the principles of democracy. In order to ensure freedom and, at the same time, take into account the values of the majority it is necessary, in our view, to determine in which areas of society – public or private – the values of the majority and of the minority should be present. In the private sphere, the freedom of moral choice should be as complete as possible. Here a person can make a moral choice at his or her own discretion, even act in a way that is contrary to public morality. In other words, a person should not be discriminated against if, for example, he cheats on his wife. This corresponds to the words of the Apostle Paul: 'Who are you, condemning the servant of another? Before his own master he stands or falls. And he will rise, for God is strong to make him stand' (Rom. 14:4). The only things that can be limited in the private sphere are moral choices which can cause injury to another member of society. However, in the public sphere of any state only those values shared by a majority of the people should be allowed to be disseminated and receive public support. The modern democratic state recognises this practice. For example, in some democratic countries there is a ban on the establishment of Nazi parties. In so doing, these restrictions do not intrude into the sphere of personal belief. A person can hold Nazi beliefs, but he may never preach them in society.

The possibility of restrictions in the application of human rights is already defined in the sources of international law in this area. Thus, Article 29, paragraph 2 of the 1948 Declaration of Human Rights states that: 'In exercising their rights and freedoms, everyone shall be subject only to such limitations as are determined by law solely for the purpose of securing due recognition and respect for human rights and freedoms of others and of meeting the just requirements of morality, public order and general welfare in a democratic society.' Thus, enshrined in the Declaration is the idea that human rights cannot be an absolute measure, but should be consistent with a number of parameters.

In a normal democratic state, one or another system of values is strengthened by debate in which various ideological groups should participate without limitation. They represent their point of view, and the majority agrees with it or rejects it. Today, we are often faced with the distortion of this principle, especially in international organisations. People having their own private views, the inherent minority, seek by means of international and national mechanisms to impose their worldview on the majority. When recurrent battles are engaged for the rights of minorities, in many cases what is at stake is not any threat to the life and happiness of these people, but the desire to impose their way of thinking and living on the majority.

In this regard, I would like to point to several problems common to many secular countries where the majority of the population belongs to the Christian culture. Under pressure from the views of religious minorities or secular circles, representing the minority, Christian symbols are removed from public places. Goodbye to Christmas trees, cribs, tables of the Ten Commandments and crosses on the flags of many European states. Others support banning the teaching of religious subjects in schools, not because anyone is forced to study them – virtually everywhere these subjects are taught on a voluntary basis – but because someone is haunted by the fact that most people willingly associate with the bases of their religious culture. In the same vein, certain people protest when the authorities meet with Christian leaders, or with religious leaders in general. The State, whose task it is to protect and preserve the cultural and spiritual heritage of the country, frequently denies this heritage in favour of the view of minorities who no longer feel beholden to it and who invent new occasions to combat what they hold up as discrimination.

A similar situation arises in the moral area, when no restrictions are placed on promoting immoral lifestyles. Of course, people of non-traditional sexual orientation should not be subjected to insults and attacks. But neither should we seek to impose a positive attitude toward homosexual relations through the school and the media, or allow such people to adopt children or teach their lifestyle. Because teaching and adoption is not just about the rights of gays, it is also about the rights of the other people whom they want to adopt or whom they intend to teach. Recently, associations defending the rights of sexual minorities have been becoming more aggressive in their slogans. Why are gay parades – in conflict with the morality of most people – imposed with so much energy on the inhabitants of the majority of European cities? What's next? A requirement to legalise paedophilia? Here too they will tell us that this is human rights. In the Netherlands there is already a political party that stands for that freedom.

The Orthodox Church today offers a return to the understanding of the role of human rights in public life as it was laid down in 1948. Moral standards can legitimately serve as a barrier to the imposition of human rights in the public sphere, whenever this is detrimental to the moral level of society. Of course, such restrictions must be clear and understandable to society. In the meantime, we are confronted only with the fact that pastors who speak out against the promotion of a homosexual lifestyle are clapped into jail. The creation of such barriers and restrictions calls for dialogue with religious organisations which uphold the standards of traditional morality at both national and international levels. Often even this democratic right is denied to religious organisations, at times under the guise of seemingly plausible premises. One technique is to bring the topic of the dialogue of civilisations into the discussion of inter-faith relations. We have seen this in particular in the wake of 11 September 2001, with people trying to sell the idea that the origin of inter-cultural tension lies in the inability of religious traditions to live in peace and good neigh-bourliness. Many are the would-be intermediaries, including people far from faith, who are quick to suggest recipes for cohabitation of different religions in the same society. All these ideas, in fact, boil down to the need, in their eyes, to minimise the influence of religion in the public sphere and deny it a voice in public debate, under the excuse of multiculturalism of the contemporary world. For the representatives of religious traditions, such conclusions look like ideological tricks to justify refusing the world's religious traditions an equal right of say in the formation of international legal norms.

Modern international organisations should make a serious step towards openness not only in the direction of secular civil society, but also of religious organisations. Within the UN framework such a step could be the creation of an Inter-Religious Council or Assembly, where representatives of the world's major religious communities can discuss values and socio-political issues. This would ensure that international institutions are not utilised to impose the views of the minority onto the majority of the population of the planet, which adheres to traditional, religiously-grounded morality. Otherwise, you will witness the further alienation of the traditional religious com-munities from the secular reading of human rights.

As I have said, the fact is that the dialogue of civilisations is neither a commonplace nor a nice-sounding slogan. It is a complex matter which can not be reduced simply to inculcating into religious people the norms of modern social life. If the secular world were to abandon its paternalistic approach to inter-faith dialogue and its self-appointed right to judge religions and we were all to sit at a round table on equal terms, then we would have the real dialogue without which it is impossible to build a just and secure world in the context of globalisation.

Chapter 13

INTER-RELATIONSHIP OF HUMAN RIGHTS AND RELIGIOUS AND CULTURAL TRADITIONS

Address to the conference 'Human Rights and National Identity',
organised by the Department for External Church Relations of the
Moscow Patriarchate and the Konrad Adenauer Foundation, Moscow,
18 April 2007

In examining this topic I believe we must begin by asking ourselves whether it is possible for the public sphere to be neutral when it comes to the bases and directions of human values. By public sphere I am referring to the activities of government institutions, social groups or individuals which have an influence on all or part of society. This definition already implies that the public space cannot be neutral, because any activity is planned and implemented on the basis of certain ideas and objectives. Legislation or policy-making cannot but take into account the values that exist in society. Similarly the development of culture, education and science is directed by value attitudes. The test for any modern society is its ability to live in a situation of multiple interacting value systems. Obviously it is very important to define the place and role of each more or less significant system of values in the public space. This is necessary for social stability, given the means, including those of coercion, that the public sphere has at its disposal.

What do I mean by means of coercion? In its legislative and political activities, the State imposes sanctions for non-performance of certain rules. Both the media and the educational system in turn use means of propaganda and persuasion based on the laws of psychology. It has to be said that the impact of the media and education on people is frequently associated with the adoption of certain standards of thought and behaviour, as well as concepts such as fashion. Fashion is a behavioural standard, and nobody can say that fashion and its standards of thought and behaviour arise spontane- ously. It is obvious that they are formed under the influence of, among other things, the media. Today the media has a huge impact on society, offering certain standards of conduct and educating the younger generation. This power over the minds is not primitive, as it was during Soviet times, when one thing was forbidden, another allowed, and people felt unfree. Man can be controlled without inducing in him a sense of protest, by presenting him behavioural and attitudinal standards in the wrappings of modern culture. And then he will himself manage his feelings and direct his actions in accord- ance with the proposed system.

At the same time the development of technical means of registra- tion is gradually leading to increased control over human life. In these circumstances, the imposition on the majority of values adhered to by a narrow group of people can lead to disaster. One way to avoid this is by society wisely determining which value systems are permitted to be present in the public sphere, and which only in the private sphere.

I would like to illustrate this thesis of mine with a concrete example. In January last year, the European Parliament adopted a resolution on homophobia in Europe. In particular, article five urges EU member states to combat homophobia in schools, universities, the media, as well as through administrative, legal and legislative means. In fact, this has already led to a situation in which, in some countries, people may not express negative attitudes towards homo- sexuality in the public sphere. If they do, they may be deprived of high political office, as was Buttiglione, or jailed, as was Pastor Green in Sweden. We are aware of other examples where people have come under pressure for expressing the view that homosexual activity is sinful. In such situations, the values and views of a minority are imposed on the majority via the public space. It may be right to leave people the freedom to choose their sexuality in the private sphere, but it is wrong to promote as natural in the public space a form of sexual behaviour that the majority of people do not agree with.

We recognise that many representative of the Western world are confronted with this and many similar problems. For example, there are cases where, under pressure from the minority, Christmas trees have been removed from public places and institutions, as have crucifixes, and the Christian names of the feast days on which heads of state present their traditional greetings to the people. Only too often, the views of religious organisations are ignored in important decisions affecting the interests of society. As a rule, representatives of the West argue that these problems can be resolved only by reference to human rights, with no other values to be taken into account. Since 1991, we, the citizens of Russia and other CIS countries, have been able not only to watch how human rights are applied in Western countries, but also to acquire our own experience of their implementation. Our experience shows that the above problems are not solved, and even, on the contrary, aggravated, if human rights are the only values in a society.

If human rights are the only value in a society, they turn into dictatorship, as I have pointed to with the example of the demands of sexual minorities. However, this does not mean that our experience fundamentally rejects human rights. On the contrary, we believe that the mechanism of human rights must be maintained and developed, because it helps to build the proper relationship between State and society, between man and man. It sets a limit on the omnipotence of the State machine, as well as inspiring everyone to respect the other person. Last year, the World Russian People's Council adopted the Declaration on Dignity and Human Rights. It talks about the need to develop human rights activities in a way that is attentive to the problems and needs of ordinary people. 'We are ready to co-operate with the state and all well-intended entities to secure the rights of humanity. This collaboration should especially focus on preserving the rights of nations and ethnic groups to their individual religion, language, and culture; upholding freedom of conscience and the right of believers to their way of life; standing against ethnic or racially motivated crime; protecting individuals against tyranny from governments or employers; caring for the rights of military personnel; protecting the rights of children; working for the rights of prisoners and the institutionalised; sheltering the victims of terrorism; preventing totalitarian control over private lives and personal faiths; and assisting the victims of crime, corruption, human trafficking, prostitution, drug abuse, and gambling addiction.'

However, in our understanding, human rights can be effective only when society also supports other values that are of equal importance to the majority of society. In the same Declaration, the World Russian People's Council said in this regard: 'There are values which are no less important than human rights. These values include faith, morality, a sense of the sacred, and one's homeland. When these values and the realisation of human rights clash, then society, the state, and the law should work to harmonise them. We must not allow situations to occur in which the upholding of human rights tramples upon religious or moral traditions, insults religious or national feelings or sacred objects, or threatens our homeland's existence.'

In our view, human rights as absolute values should be consistent with other, no less important, values: spirituality, morality and love of the homeland. This idea is there in the Universal Declaration of Human Rights, which states, in Article 29, paragraph 2, that: 'In exercising their rights and freedoms, everyone shall be subject only to such limitations as are determined by law solely for the purpose of securing due recognition and respect for human rights and freedoms of others and of meeting the just requirements of morality, public order and general welfare in a democratic society.' Thus, even if politicians seem to have forgotten the fact, the Universal Declaration itself contains the idea that human rights can not be an absolute measure, but should be consonant with a number of other values.

Our position on the need to reaffirm other values should not, however, be understood as a call for the State or society to act in an arbitrary manner towards the individual. The call is rather for the patterns of lives of the majority of individuals to be integrated into public and social life. This means that anything that fails to take account of those values, even if justified by human rights, should be kept out of the public sphere. Of course, when it comes to values, absolute consensus with all forces of society is impossible, but it can be achieved with a greater part of society. Therefore, the political significance of the debate on human rights initiated by the Russian Orthodox Church is not a desire to eliminate human rights from public life. It is rather the desire to move towards building a real democracy, not only in Russia but also in the world. Real democracy means hearing and following the voice of the majority of citizens, especially with regard to values.

Chapter 14

HUMAN RIGHTS AND INTERCULTURAL DIALOGUE

Speaking at a panel discussion on 'Human Rights and Intercultural Dialogue' at the 7th session of the UN Human Rights Council, Geneva, 18 March 2008

The Human Rights Council is a young structure within the galaxy of United Nations structures. It is, however, backed by the long experience of this authoritative organisation in the interpretation and implementation of human rights. The Council has significant opportunities to bring new partners into the discussion on the issues which lie within its competence. Among these, religious organisations will, I hope, occupy a worthy place.

Certainly, human rights are an important institution of our contemporary social structure. The attractiveness of the concept is based on the simple and accessible idea that central to social life is a concern for the welfare of each individual. It is precisely this idea that Christianity brought to European culture. Christianity constantly proclaims the availability of salvation for every person, regardless of national or social origin, while at the same time emphasising the uniqueness and value of each individual in God's plan for the world.

Christians cannot remain uninvolved in the subsequent fate of this important message to humanity, even if expressed in the secular language of human rights. It is important that this institution continues to serve the good of every person and of society as a whole.

However, in the opinion of many Orthodox Christians, in the development and application of human rights certain trends are today gaining momentum that can potentially jeopardise the attainment of this lofty goal.

First and foremost, the development of the institution of human rights is increasingly falling under the monopolistic influence of a limited range of propositions concerning human nature that are not shared by the majority of the inhabitants of our planet. Often, international organisations dealing with human rights issues base their conclusions on the views of a narrow circle of experts, officials, or loud, but well-organised, minorities. Many nation-states are also strongly influenced by these players and in so doing lose the ability to translate the original values on which the lives of their own people are structured into their political activity and legislation.

Characteristically, of the most common and widely used concepts in connection with the topic of human rights – human dignity – there is today no clear and commonly accepted understanding. It is used as a kind of axiom, even though discussion of its contents is long overdue. Key to this understanding is how we understand man, and thus his rights.

For Orthodox Christians, it is clear that human dignity is inconceivable without the religious and spiritual and moral dimension. At the same time the need to ensure the applicability of human rights for people of different ideologies is often used to vindicate distancing human rights from religion. As a result, religious belief is declared a private affair and is not considered as a source of modern law, including human rights. This happens despite the fact that, according to widespread estimates, approximately 80 per cent of the world's population are religious people.

On the contrary, what we hear is the demand for the subordination of religious beliefs to norms born on the soil of non-religious ideas. This leads to the dominance of agnostic or even materialistic approaches to life that justly annoys believers. And in practice this leads to exclusion from the public sphere of religious rituals, symbols and ideas. Even a favourite Christian holiday – Christmas – has in many Western countries lost its name. Today the authorities congratulate the people at non-Christian seasonal festivals. Human rights are also used to justify insult to, and distortion of, religious symbols and beliefs. Following the same approach people now seek to replace the teaching of the foundations of their own religion in schools with a general introductory course on the various religions.

In short, we are seeing a secular approach that leads people to abandon the expression of their faith in public life. This leads to the construction of a non-religious society, which can not enjoy the support of any truly religious person.

Furthermore, we observe the strong influence on language standards, guidelines and programmes in the field of human rights activities, of extreme feminist views and gay attitudes which are destructive to the institution of family and population reproduction. It is not for us to judge the lifestyle choices of different people, but why should their views be forcibly imposed, through the legal system, on other people that do not share them? Recently it was announced that the UK was banning Roman Catholic adoption agencies that refuse to consider same-sex couples as potential candidates for adoptive parents.

We can not accept approaches to the role of men and women, to male-female relationships, to relationships between parents and children, or the status of same-sex unions, which appear to fail to take into account the opinion of believers.

The view of abortion as a woman's right has led us to a situation in which international organisations are deaf and blind to the right to life of a conceived child. Today there are no references to ethics when experimentation takes place with human embryos. Even more surprising is the proposal to amend the corpus of human rights law on euthanasia. Human rights, which begin with the fundamental right to life, may in the near future be on the side of death.

At the same time, serious questions arise when it comes to the application of human rights. One problem in this area relates to the interpretation of the concept of freedom. The body of human rights strengthens people's opportunities to act in certain ways at their discretion. In other words, they protect the freedom of choice, but say nothing about human responsibility. As a result, man is free, but left defenceless against evil. What do we mean here by freedom from evil? In our view, it is described in the language of moral norms. In his speech to the Parliamentary Assembly of the Council of Europe last year, Patriarch Alexy II offered an understanding of morality as a positive liberty: 'Morality is freedom in action. This freedom is realised as a result of responsible choice, placing limits on ourselves for our own good and that of society.'

I would like to recall that the UN standards, which are based, *inter alia*, on the Universal Declaration of Human Rights of 1948, also place limits on the freedom of choice for the sake of 'meeting the just requirements of morality'. Unfortunately, in the Charter of Fundamental Rights of the European Union this restrictive setting is omitted.

In many countries, under the pretext of freedom, we are seeing the active development of a commercial industry filling society with propaganda for an immoral lifestyle. We believe that people should have the right to be shielded from the preaching of violence, the consumption of drugs and alcohol, gambling and sexual promiscuity.

In our view, human rights must not conflict with moral norms that are recognised by most people as a desirable behaviour. If human rights become supportive of moral relativism in society, they become something alien to believers.

The subject of human rights also raises the issue of whether rights-protection systems can take different forms in different countries of the world. Yes, human rights have a universal application. However, it is perfectly feasible that they be embodied in a manner that reflects the cultural sensitivities of one or another nation. In some countries people are more religious than in others. Here religion can and should play a more prominent role in the formation and implementation of human rights. In addition, every nation has its own historical experience, cultural traditions and thought systems. One can not ignore these realities in constructing a national human rights system. In this respect certain countries act in a totally undemocratic fashion by considering their particular system of implementation of human rights as universally applicable. Directly or indirectly they seek to impose their standards on other peoples or to set themselves up as the sole arbiters of human rights. I would suggest that in this case the only acceptable dialogue is one which excludes the 'teacher–pupil' situation. Finally, I cannot keep silent about the harmful effect of such double standards on the reputation of human rights activities. Not infrequently, human rights are used by some countries as a tool for their national interests. This is particularly evident in the conflict regions of the planet. The most recent example is the situation in Kosovo and Metochia. These cases stoke up anger in various parts of the world and sow prejudice against human rights.

Summarising the above, I would say the following. Today, everyone is talking about the clash of civilisations or cultures, but what we are really dealing with is a conflict of approaches, one based on a religious world view and the other on a secular one. For some reason, it is widely believed that a non-religious and morally neutral approach best expresses the universal aspirations of humanity and deals with various contradictions in the world. But to do so is to forget that the religious and moral dimension of human life is universal and applies to all peoples.

The religious approach, as I have tried to show, attaches great importance to the social role of religion, as well as to maintaining a unified moral system in society. It is precisely on this basis that both international law, including human rights, and national legislation should be structured. Otherwise, the alienation and opposition of a large part of humanity towards ongoing global processes will only increase. The non-confrontational way out of the current situation is to hold intensive dialogue.

The Russian Orthodox Church is currently in the process of structuring a comprehensive approach to human rights. This summer, if all goes to plan, a document on this subject will be adopted by our church's highest governing body – the Council of Bishops. From the experience of inter-Christian and inter-religious dialogue we know that other Christian denominations and world religions have also developed approaches to the topic of human rights. It would be good to create opportunities for these views to be heard on the platform of the Human Rights Council and at the UN in general.

In 2006, Moscow hosted a summit of world religious leaders. The ensuing debate showed that, despite the differences that exist, religious figures acknowledged the important role of religion in society and noted the closeness of the fundamental ethical norms of major world religions. In my opinion, this could provide the necessary meeting point between different civilisations in the modern world.

The summit made a proposal to create a platform for religious dialogue in the UN. An appeal in this direction was addressed to the leaders of the Group of Eight. Russia, as is known, supported this idea. Last year, at the 62nd UN General Assembly, its foreign minister proposed that a consultative council of religions be set up with special UN status. I very much hope that other interested countries will be able to support this reasonable initiative by religious leaders, which would give new impetus to dialogue on human rights at the global level.

Appendix

THE RUSSIAN ORTHODOX CHURCH'S BASIC TEACHING ON HUMAN DIGNITY, FREEDOM AND RIGHTS

Published by the Bishops' Council of the Russian Orthodox Church in June 2008

Introduction

Throughout human history the understanding of what constitutes the human being has considerably influenced the way in which people have organised their private and public life. Despite the profound differences existing between particular civilisations and cultures, every one of them has some ideas of human rights and obligations.

In the world today there is a widespread conviction that the human rights institution in itself can promote in the best possible way the development of human personality and social organisation. At the same time, human rights protection is often used as a plea to realise ideas which in essence radically disagree with Christian teaching. Christians have found themselves in a situation where public and social structures can force and often have already forced them to think and act contrary to God's commandments, thus obstructing their way towards the most important goal in human life, which is deliverance from sin and finding salvation.

In this situation the Church, on the basis of Holy Scriptures and the Holy Tradition, has to recall the basic affirmations of Christian teaching on the human person and to assess the theory of human rights and its implementation.

I. Human dignity as a religious and ethical category

I. 1. The human rights theory is based on human dignity as its fundamental notion. This is the reason why the need arises to set forth the Church's view of human dignity.

According to the Biblical revelation, God not only created human nature but also endowed it with qualities in His image and after His likeness (cf. Gen. 1:26). It is the only ground which makes it possible to assert that human nature has an inherent dignity. St Gregory the Theologian, speaking about human dignity as related to the act of divine creation, wrote: 'God has endowed all human beings so generously so that by distributing His gifts equally He may also show the equal dignity of our nature and the abundance of His grace' (Oration 14, *On the Love for the Poor*).

The incarnation of God the Word showed that human nature did not lose its dignity even after the Fall, for the image of God in it remained indelible, which means that an opportunity remained for restoring human life in the fullness of its original perfection. This is embedded also in the liturgical texts of the Orthodox Church: 'I am an image of thy glory ineffable, though I bear the brands of transgressions ... O thou who of old didst call me into being from nothingness, and didst honour me with thine image divine, but because I had transgressed thy commandments hast returned me again unto the earth from which I was taken: Restore thou me to that image, and to my pristine beauty' (Troparia from the *Order of the Funeral of the Dead*).

The fact that the Lord Jesus Christ assumed human nature in its fullness except for sin (cf. Heb. 4:15) shows that this dignity does not apply to the distortions resulting from the Fall.

I. 2. In Orthodoxy the dignity and ultimate worth of every human person are derived from the image of God, while dignified life is related to the notion of God's likeness achieved through God's grace by efforts to overcome sin and to seek moral purity and virtue. Therefore, the human being as bearing the image of God should not exult in this lofty dignity, for it is not his own achievement but a gift of God. Nor should he use it to justify his weaknesses or vices, but rather understand his responsibility for the direction and way of his life. Clearly, the idea of responsibility is integral to the very notion of dignity.

Therefore, in the Eastern Christian tradition the notion of 'dignity' has first of all a moral meaning, while the ideas of what is dignified and what is not are bound up with the moral or amoral actions of a person and with the inner state of his soul. Considering the state of human nature darkened by sin, it is important that things dignified and undignified should be clearly distinguished in the life of a person.

I. 3. Dignified is a life lived according to its original calling laid down in the nature of the human being created for participation in the good life of God. St Gregory of Nyssa affirms: 'If the Deity is the fullness of good, and this is His image, then the image finds its resemblance to the Archetype in being filled with all good' (*On the Creation of Man*, Chapter XVI).

Human life therefore lies in seeking 'God's likeness in all virtue so far as it is possible for man', as St John of Damascus says in his *Exact Exposition of the Orthodox Faith*. The patristic tradition describes this elicitation of the image of God as deification.

The God-given dignity is confirmed by a moral principle present in every person and discerned in the voice of conscience. This is what St Paul writes about it in his Epistle to the Romans: 'The work of the law is written in their hearts, their conscience also bearing witness, and their thoughts the mean while accusing or else excusing one another' (2:15).

Thus moral norms inherent in humanity just as moral norm set forth in the divine revelation reveal God's design for human beings and their calling. These norms are guidelines for a good life worthy of God-created humanity. It was the Lord Jesus Christ who showed the greatest model of such a life to the world.

I. 4. A life in sin is unworthy of the human person as it destroys him and inflicts damage on others and the world around him. Sin overturns the hierarchy of relations in human nature. Instead of having his body controlled by the spirit, in sin the human person submits to the flesh – the situation brought into focus by St John Chrysostom: 'We upset the order and an onset of evil occurred so as to oblige us to follow the bidding of the flesh' (Discourse 12 on the *Book of the Genesis*).

A life according to the law of the flesh is contrary to God's commandments and it does not agree with the moral principle laid down by God in human nature. Under the influence of sin, a person in his relations with others acts as an egoist preoccupied with indulging himself at the expense of others. Such a life endangers the individual, society and the surrounding nature as it violates the harmony of existence and results in spiritual and physical suffering, illnesses and vulnerability in the face of consequences brought about by the erosion of the environment. A morally undignified life does not ruin the God-given dignity ontologically but darkens it so much as to make it hardly discernable. This is why it takes so much effort of will to discern and even admit the natural dignity of a villain or a tyrant.

I. 5. A special importance in restoring a person to his appropriate dignity belongs to repentance based on the awareness of his sin and desire to change his life. A repentant person admits that his thoughts, words or actions are not consonant with the God-given dignity and acknowledges his indignity before God and the Church. Repentance does not humiliate a person but rather gives him a powerful stimulus for seeking spiritual self-cultivation, making a creative change in his life, preserving the purity of the God-given dignity and growing in it.

For this very reason the patristic and ascetic thought and the whole liturgical tradition of the Church refer more to human indignity caused by sin than to human dignity. Thus the Prayer of St Basil the Great said by an Orthodox Christian before the Holy Communion reads: 'Wherefore I, although unworthy both of heaven and of earth and of this temporary life, even I, a wretched sinner who had given myself over to every evil desire, despair not of salvation, though I have been wholly subject to sin, a slave to passion, and have defiled thine image within me, who am thy creation and thy work; but trusting in thine infinite compassion, draw nigh unto thee'.

According to the Orthodox tradition, a human being preserves his God-given dignity and grows in it only if he lives in accordance with moral norms because these norms express the primordial and there-fore authentic human nature not darkened by sin. Thus there is a direct link between human dignity and morality. Moreover, the acknowledgement of personal dignity implies the assertion of per-sonal responsibility.

II. Freedom of choice and freedom from evil

II. 1. The image of God can be either darkened or illumined depending on the self-determination of a free individual, while the natural dignity becomes either more apparent in his life or obliterated by sin. The result is directly dependent on the self-determination of an individual.

Freedom is one of the manifestations of God in human nature. According to St Gregory of Nyssa, 'Man became Godlike and blessed, being honoured with freedom (αὐτεξουσίῳ)' (*Sermon on the Dead*). For this reason the Church in her pastoral practice and spiritual guidance takes so much care of the inner world of a person and his freedom of choice. Subjection of human will to any external authority through manipulation or violence is seen as a violation of the order established by God.

At the same time, freedom of choice is not an absolute or ultimate value. God has put it at the service of human well-being. Exercising it, a person should not harm either himself or those around him. But due to the power of sin inherent in the fallen human nature, no human effort is sufficient to achieve genuine goodness. By his own example St Paul testifies to what is characteristic of every person: 'I do not understand what I do. For what I want to do I do not do, but what I hate I do … It is no longer I myself who do it, but it is sin living in me' (Rom. 7:15, 17).

Therefore, a human being cannot dispense with God's help and close co-operation with Him as He alone is the source of every good thing.

Having rejected God to rely only on themselves, the first people found themselves under the sway of the destructive forces of evil and death and handed down this dependence to their ancestors. Having abused the freedom of choice, human beings lost another freedom – ἐλευθερία, the freedom to live in goodness that they had had in their primordial state. It is this freedom that the Lord Jesus Christ restores to them: 'So if the Son sets you free, you will be free indeed (ἐλεύθεροι) (John 8:36). It is impossible to find freedom from sin without the mysterious unity of man with the transfigured nature of

Christ that takes place in the Sacrament of Baptism (cf. Rom. 6:3–6; Col. 3:10) and becomes ever stronger through life in the Church, the Body of Christ (cf. Col. 1:24).

Holy Scripture speaks also of the need for a person to make his own efforts in order to be delivered from sin: 'Stand firm, then, and do not let yourselves be burdened again by a yoke of slavery' (Gal. 5:1). The same testimony is given by the practical experience of a great number of holy men and women who pursued spiritual feats and reconfirmed the possibility for every person to transform his life. The fruits of human spiritual efforts however will manifest themselves fully only in the universal resurrection when 'our vile body' will be fashioned 'like unto his glorious body' (Phil. 3:21).

II. 2. The Lord Jesus Christ says, 'And ye shall know the truth, and the truth shall make you free ... Whosoever committeth sin is the servant of sin' (John 8:32, 34). This means that only those are truly free who take the path of righteous life and seek communion with God, the source of absolute truth. But the abuse of freedom and the choice of a false, immoral, way of life will ultimately destroy the very freedom of choice as it leads the will to slavery by sin. It is God alone as the source of freedom who can maintain it in a human being. Those who do not wish to part with sin give away their freedom to the devil, the enemy of God and the father of evil and captivity. While recognising the value of freedom of choice, the Church affirms that this freedom will inevitably disappear if the choice is made in favour of evil. Evil and freedom are incompatible.

In human history, the choice made by people and societies in favour of evil led to the loss of freedom and to the enormous loss of lives. And today humanity may follow the same path if such absolutely vicious things as abortion, suicide, lechery, perversion, destruction of the family, the worship of cruelty and violence are no longer given a proper moral assessment and justified by a distorted understanding of human freedom.

The weakness of the human rights institution lies in the fact that, while defending the freedom (αὐτεξούσιον) of choice, it tends to increasingly ignore the moral dimension of life and the freedom from sin (ἐλευθερία). The social system should be guided by both freedoms, harmonising their exercise in the public sphere. One of these freedoms cannot be defended while the other is neglected. Free adherence to goodness and the truth is impossible without the freedom of choice, just as a free choice loses it value and meaning if it is made in favour of evil.

III. Human rights in the Christian worldview and in the life of society

III. 1. Every individual is endowed by God with dignity and freedom. The use of this freedom for evil purposes however will inevitably lead to the derogation of one's own dignity and humiliation of the dignity of others. A society should establish mechanisms restoring harmony between human dignity and freedom. In social life, the concept of human rights and morality can and must serve this purpose. At the same time these two notions are bound up at least by the fact that morality, that is, the ideas of sin and virtue, always precede law, which has actually arisen from these ideas. That is why any erosion of morality will ultimately lead to the erosion of legality.

The concept of human rights has undergone a long historical evolution and precisely for this reason cannot be made absolute in their today's understanding. It is necessary to give a clear definition to Christian values with which human rights should be harmonised.

III. 2. **Human rights cannot be superior to the values of the spiritual world.** A Christian puts his faith in God and his communion with Him above his earthly life. It is inadmissible and dangerous therefore to interpret human rights as the ultimate and universal foundation of societal life to which religious views and practice should be subjected. No reference whatsoever to the freedom of expression and creative work can justify the public defilement of objects, symbols or notions cherished by believers.

Not a divine institution, human rights should not come into inflict with the Divine Revelation. For most of Christendom the category of doctrinal and moral tradition is no less important than the idea of individual freedom and the individual should reconcile his freedom with it. For many people in various parts of the world it is not so much secularised standards of human rights as the creed and traditions that have the ultimate authority in their social life and interpersonal relations.

No human institutions, including various forms and mechanisms of the socio-political order, can in themselves make people's life more moral and perfect and eradicate evil and suffering. It is important to remember that public and social forces have a real power and duty to stop evil in its social manifestations, but they cannot prevail over sin as its cause. The essential struggle with evil is carried out in the depth of the human spirit and can succeed only if it is waged through personal religious life: 'Our struggle is not against flesh and blood, but against the rulers, against the authorities, against the powers of this dark world and against the spiritual forces of evil in the heavenly realms' (Eph. 6:12).

In Orthodoxy, there is an immutable conviction that in ordering its life a society should take into account not only human interests and wishes but also the divine truth, the eternal moral law given by the Lord and working in the world no matter whether the will of particular people or people's communities agree with it or not. For an Orthodox Christian, this law sealed in Holy Scriptures stands above any other rules, for it is by this law that God will judge the individual and nations standing before His throne (cf. Rev. 20:12).

III. 3. The development and implementation of the human rights concept should be harmonised with the norms of morality, with the ethical principle laid down by God in human nature and discernable in the voice of conscience.

Human rights cannot be a reason for coercing Christians into violation of God's commandments. The Orthodox Church believes it inadmissible that the believer's view of the human being, family, communal life and church practice should be subjected to a non-religious understanding of human rights. Christians should respond to such attempts as Ss Peter and John did, saying, 'Judge for yourselves whether it is right in God's sight to obey you rather than God' (Acts 4:19).

It is inadmissible to introduce in the area of human rights the norms that obliterate or altogether cancel both the Gospel and natural morality. The Church sees a great danger in the legislative and public support given to various vices, such as sexual lechery and perversions, the worship of profit and violence. It is equally inadmissible to elevate to a norm such immoral and inhumane actions towards the human being as abortion, euthanasia, use of human embryos in medicine, experiments changing a person's nature and the like.

Unfortunately, society has seen the emergence of legislative norms and political practices which not only allow of such actions but also create preconditions for them by imposing them through the mass media, education and healthcare systems, advertising, commerce and services. Moreover, believers, who consider such things to be sinful, are forced to accept sin as admissible or are subjected to discrimination and persecution.

According to the law in many countries, actions harmful to others are punishable. However, life experience shows that the damage inflicted by a person on himself tends to spread to those around him, those who are tied with him by the bonds of kinship, friendship, neighbourhood, common work or citizenship. The individual is responsible for the consequences of sin since his choice for evil has a baneful influence on his neighbours and on the whole of God's creation.

The human being is called to good works by virtue of his dignity. The individual is obliged to take care of the world and people around him. He should seek in his life to do good and to teach good, not evil: 'Anyone who breaks one of the least of these commandments and teaches others to do the same will be called least in the kingdom of heaven, but whoever practices and teaches these commands will be called great in the kingdom of heaven' (Matt. 5:19).

III. 4. **Human rights should not contradict love for one's homeland and neighbours.** The Creator has laid down in human nature the need for communication and unity, saying, 'It is not good for the man to be alone' (Gen. 2:18). The love of a person for his family and other loved ones cannot but spread to his people and the country in which he lives. It is not accidental that the Orthodox tradition traces patriotism back to the words of Christ the Saviour Himself: 'Greater love has no one than this, that he lay down his life for his friends' (John 15:13).

The acknowledgment of individual rights should be balanced with the assertion of people's responsibility before one another. The extremes of individualism and collectivism cannot promote a harmonious order in a society's life. They lead to degradation of the personality, moral and legal nihilism, growing crime, civil inaction and people's mutual alienation.

The spiritual experience of the Church however has shown that the tension between private and public interests can be overcome only if human rights and freedoms are harmonised with moral values and, most importantly, only if the life of the individual and society is invigorated by love. It is love that removes all the contradictions between the individual and those around him, making him capable of enjoying his freedom fully while taking care of his neighbours and homeland.

Actions aimed at respect for human rights and improvement of social and economic relations and institutions will not be truly successful if the religious and cultural traditions of countries and nations are ignored.

Some civilisations ought not to impose their own way of life on other civilisations under the pretext of human rights protection. The human rights activity should not be put at the service of interests of particular countries. The struggle for human rights becomes fruitful only if it contributes to the spiritual and material welfare of both the individual and society.

III. 5. **The realisation of human rights should not lead to the degradation of the environment and depletion of natural resources.** The rejection of divinely-revealed guiding lines in the life of both the individual and society leads not only to disorder in interpersonal relations but also to people's disastrous clash with nature, which has been given to human beings by God to own (cf. Gen. 1:28). The unlimited desire to satisfy material needs, especially excessive and artificial, is essentially sinful, for it leads to the impoverishment of both the soul and its environment. It should not be forgotten that the natural riches of the earth are not only the property of humanity but first of all the creation of God: 'The earth is the Lord's, and the fullness thereof; the world, and they that dwell therein' (Ps. 24:1).

The recognition of human rights does not mean that people can squander natural resources in favour of their egoistic interests. Human dignity is inseparable from the calling of the human beings to take care of God's world (cf. Gen. 2:15), to be moderate in meeting their needs, to preserve the richness, variety and beauty of nature. These truths should be taken into account with all seriousness by society and State in defining the basic goals of socio-economic and material-technical development. It should be borne in mind that not only the present but also the future generations have the right to use the natural wealth given by the Creator.

From the point of view of the Orthodox Church the political and legal institution of human rights can promote the good goals of protecting human dignity and contribute to the spiritual and ethical development of the personality. To make it possible the implementation of human rights should not come into conflict with God-established moral norms and traditional morality based on them. One's human rights cannot be set against the values and interests of one's homeland, community and family. The exercise of human rights should not be used to justify any encroachment on religious holy symbols things, cultural values and the identity of a nation. Human rights cannot be used as a pretext for inflicting irretrievable damage on nature.

IV. Human dignity and freedom in the system of human rights

IV. 1. There are various traditions of interpretation of rights and freedoms and national peculiarities in implementing them. The modern system of human rights is widely accepted and has a tendency for even greater specification. There is no commonly accepted classification of rights and freedoms. Various legal schools unite them in groups according to various criteria. The Church, by virtue of her basic calling, suggests considering rights and freedoms in the perspective of their possible role in creating favourable external conditions for the improvement of personality on its way to salvation.

IV. 2. **The right to life**. Life is a gift of God to human beings. The Lord Jesus Christ preaches: 'I have come that they may have life, and have it to the full' (John 10:10). God gave the Prophet Moses a commandment that 'you shall not kill'. Orthodoxy does not accept terrorism and condemns it, as armed aggression and criminal violence just as all other forms of the criminal taking away of human life.

At the same time, life is not restricted to temporal limits in which the secular worldview and its legal system place the individual. Christianity testifies that temporal life, precious in itself, acquires fullness and absolute meaning in the perspective of eternal life. Priority therefore should be given not to the efforts to preserve temporal life by all means but to the desire to order it in such a way as to enable people to work together with God for preparing their souls for eternity.

The Word of God teaches that giving one's earthly life for Christ and the gospel (cf. Mark 8:35) and for other people will not hamper one's salvation but, quite to the contrary, will lead one to the Kingdom of Heaven (cf. John 15:13). The Church honours the feat of martyrs who served God even to death and the feat of confessors who refused to renounce Him in face of persecutions and threats. Orthodox Christians also honour the heroism of those who gave their lives in battlefield fighting for their homeland and neighbours.

At the same time the Church condemns suicide since those who commit it do not sacrifice themselves but reject life as a gift of God. In this connection the Church cannot accept the legalisation of so-called euthanasia, that is, assistance given to those who wish to die, which is actually a combination of murder and suicide.

The right to life should imply the protection of a human life from the moment of its conception. Any intrusion in the life of a developing human personality is a violation of this right. Modern international and national legal acts seal and protect the life and rights of the child, adult and senior citizen. The same logic of human life protection should be applied to the period of life from its conception to birth. The Biblical idea of the God-given value of human life from the moment of its conception is expressed in particular in the words of the holy King David: 'For You formed my inward parts; You covered me in my mother's womb ... My frame was not hidden from You, when I was made in secret, and skillfully wrought in the lowest parts of the earth. Your eyes saw my substance, being yet unformed. And in Your book they all were written, the days fashioned for me, when as yet there were none of them' (Ps. 139:13, 15–16).

While admitting that the death penalty was acceptable in the Old Testament time and there are no instructions to abolish it 'either in the Holy Scripture of the New Testament or in the Tradition or in the historical legacy of the Orthodox Church', we cannot but recall that 'the Church has often taken upon herself the duty of intercession for those condemned to death, asking mercy or mitigation of punishment for them' (*The Russian Orthodox Church's Basic Social Concept,* IX. 3).

Defending human life, the Church, whatever society's attitude to death penalty may be, is called to fulfil this duty of intercession.

IV. 3. **Freedom of conscience.** The individual can see the gift of freedom of choice first of all in the opportunity for him to choose particular philosophical guidelines for his life. As St Irenaeus of Lyons writes: 'God made man free from the beginning, possessing his own power … to obey the behests of God voluntarily, and not by God's compulsion' (*Against Heresies,* Book IV, Chapter 37).

The principle of freedom of conscience is in harmony with God's will if it protects the individual against any arbitrary treatment of his inner world, against any forcible imposition of particular convictions upon him. It is not without reason that the Russian Orthodox Church's Basic Social Concept speaks of the need 'to preserve for the individual a certain autonomous space where his conscience remains the absolute master, for it is on the free will that salvation or death, the way towards Christ or away from Christ will ultimately depend' (IV, 6).

In a secular state, the freedom of conscience, proclaimed and confirmed by law, enables the Church to preserve her identity and independence from people of other convictions and gives her a legal ground both for the immunity of her internal life and public witness to the Truth. At the same time, 'the freedom of conscience asserted as a legal principle points to the fact that society has lost religious goals and values' (BSC, III, 6).

The freedom of conscience is sometimes treated as requiring religious neutrality or indifference of a state and society. Some ideological interpretations of religious freedom insist on the need to recognise all the faiths as relative or 'equally true'. This is unacceptable for the Church which, while respecting the freedom of choice, is called to bear witness to the Truth she cherishes and to expose its misinterpretations (cf. 2 Tim. 3:15).

A society has the right to determine freely the content and amount of co-operation the State should maintain with various religious communities depending on their strength, traditional presence in a particular country or region, contribution to the history and culture of the country and on their civil attitude. At the same time, there must be equality of citizens before law regardless of their attitude to religion. The principle of freedom of conscience does not present an obstacle for partnership relations between the Church and the State in social, educational or any other socially significant activities.

The freedom of conscience cannot be used to establish total control over the life and beliefs of the individual, to destroy his private, family and social morality, to insult his religious feelings, to encroach on things he holds sacred, to damage his spiritual and cultural identity as all this distorts its very essence.

IV. 4. **The freedom of expression.** The freedom of thoughts and feelings, which presupposes the possibility for disseminating information, is a natural continuation of the freedom of ideological choice. The word is a principal means of communication between people and God and among one another. The content of communication has a serious impact on the well-being of the person and interpersonal relations in a society. The individual bears a special responsibility for his words. 'By your words you will be justified, and by your words you will be condemned' (Matt. 12:37) says Holy Scriptures. Public statements and declarations should not further the propagation of sin or generate strife and disorder in society. The word should create and support the good. It is especially dangerous to insult religious and national feelings, to distort information about the life of particular religious communities, nations, social groups and personalities. Responsibility for words has grown manifold in the modern world as it experiences a rapid development of the technologies of storing and disseminating information.

IV. 5. **The freedom of creative work.** Human creative ability is essentially a manifestation of God's image in the human being. The Church blesses creative work as it opens up new horizons for the spiritual growth of the individual and for his knowledge of the created world. Called to help reveal the potential of the personality, creative work should not justify any nihilistic attitude to culture, religion and morality. The right to self-expression for an individual or a group should not be implemented in forms insulting for the beliefs and ways of life of other members of society, and one of the main principles of communal life, namely, mutual respect for various worldview groups should be observed.

Sacrilege towards holy things cannot be justified by references to the rights of an artist, writer or journalist. Modern law normally protects not only people's life and property but also symbolical values, such as the memory of the dead, burial places, historical and cultural monuments and national symbols. This protection should be applied to the faith and things held sacred by religious people.

IV. 6. **The right to education.** The goal of a person's temporal life is to seek the likeness of God by means of virtue. Education is a means of not only learning or incorporating a person in the life of society, but also forming his personality in accordance with the design of the Creator. The right to education presupposes learning that takes into account the cultural traditions of society and the worldview of the individual and his family. As most of the world cultures are based on religion, the comprehensive education and formation of a person should include the teaching of knowledge about the religion that has created the culture in which this person lives. At the same time, his freedom of conscience should be respected.

IV. 7. **Civil and political rights.** Holy Scriptures instructs the faithful to fulfil their family and socially important obligations as obedience to Christ (cf. Luke 10–14; Eph. 5:23–33; Tit. 3:1). St Paul made use of his rights as Roman citizen on more than one occasion in order to preach the Word of God. Civil and political rights offer the individual an ample opportunity for effective service of his neighbour. Using this instrument, a citizen can make an influence on the life of society and participate in governing the State. It is on the way in which an individual uses his right to elect and to be elected, to join freely an association or a union, to use freedom of expression and beliefs that the welfare of a society depends.

The use of political and civil rights should not lead to divisions and enmity. The Orthodox tradition of conciliarity implies the preservation of the social unity on the basis of intransient moral values. The Church calls upon people to restrain their egoistic desires for the sake of the common good.

The peoples under the spiritual care of the Russian Orthodox Church have developed in their history a fruitful idea of the need for co-operation between the authorities and people. Political rights can make a valid contribution to these State-society relations. To achieve this end, civil interests should have a real representation on various levels of power and opportunities for civil action should be ensured.

People's private life, worldview and will should not become a subject of total control. Any manipulation over people's choice and their conscience by power structures, political forces and economic and media elites is dangerous for a society. Such things as compilation, concentration and use of information about any aspect of people's life without their consent are also inadmissible. Information about a person can be collected without his or her consent only in cases where it is required for the defence of the homeland, preservation of morality, protection of people's health, rights and legitimate interests or the need to investigate a crime and to exercise justice. But in these cases too, information may be collected and used in conformity with the stated aims and in accordance with law. The methods of collecting and processing information about people should not hurt the dignity of a person, restrict his freedom or turn him from a subject of public relations into an object of machine operation. The adoption of technical devices accompanying a person permanently or inseparable from his body will be even more dangerous for human freedom if used to control his personality.

IV. 8. **Socio-economic rights.** A person's earthly life is impossible without having his material needs satisfied. The Book of Acts tells the story of the first Christian community in which the level of material care for its members was especially high (cf. Acts 4:32–37; 6:1–6). The right usage of material wealth does matter in the cause of salvation. It is necessary therefore to give a clear moral dimension to such rights and freedoms as the right to property, the right to employment, the right to protection against an employer's arbitrary treatment, the freedom of enterprise and the right to dignified living standards.

The exercise of economic rights should not lead to the formation of such a society in which the use of material wealth is turned into a dominating or even the only aim of a society's existence. One of the purposes of economic and social rights is to prevent confrontational stratification of a society. Such stratification is contrary to the commandment to love one's neighbour. It creates conditions for the moral degradation of both society and the individual, generates the feeling of alienation between people and violates the principle of justice.

A society has as its important responsibility to take care of those who are unable to secure their material needs. Access to education and vital medical care should not depend on the social or economic status of a person.

IV. 9. **Collective rights.** The rights of an individual should not be destructive for the unique way of life and traditions of the family and for various religious, national and social communities. God has laid down in human nature the desire of a human being to share in communal life (cf. Gen. 2:18). In the fulfilment of God's will for the unity of the human race, an important role belongs to various forms of communal life realised in national, public and social associations, while it is in the Church, the divine-human organism, that God's commandment of love for God and the neighbour is fully revealed (cf. Matt. 22:37–39).

Communal life begins in the family. For this reason St Paul speaks of the family's participation in the Mystery of the Church (cf. Eph. 5:23–33). It is in his family that a person gains an experience of love for God and his neighbour. It is through the family that religious traditions, the social way of life and national culture of a society are handed down. The modern law should view the family as the lawful union of man and woman in which natural conditions for raising children are created. Law is also called to respect the family as an integral organism and to protect it against destruction provoked by moral decay. In safeguarding the rights of the child, the legal system should not deny his parents a special role in his education, which is inseparable from their worldview and religious experience.

It is necessary to respect other collective rights as well, such as the right to peace, the right to the environment, the right to preservation of cultural heritage and internal norms regulating the life of various communities.

Unity and inter-connection between civil and political, economic and social, individual and collective human rights can promote a harmonious order of societal life both on the national and international level. The social value and effectiveness of the entire human rights system depend on the extent to which it helps to create conditions for personal growth in the God-given dignity and relates to the responsibility of a person for his actions before God and his neighbours.

V. Principles and areas of the Russian Orthodox Church's human rights work

V. 1. From olden times till today the Orthodox Church has been engaged in intercession to the authorities for those who are unjustly convicted, humiliated, deprived or exploited. The Church extends her merciful intercession also to those who are justly punished for their crimes. The Church has repeatedly called to stop violence and mitigate morals during conflicts that flared up when the human rights to life, healthcare, freedom and property were trampled down. Finally, in the years of the godless persecution, Orthodox bishops, clergy and laity appealed to the authorities and society seeking to defend the freedom of religious confession and advocating the right of religious communities to broad participation in the life of the people.

V. 2. Today just as before, we are called to show concern, not only in word but also in deed, for the protection of human rights and dignity. At the same time, we are aware that human rights are often violated in the modern world and human dignity is trampled down not only by the State authorities but also transnational structures, economic actors, pseudo-religious groups, terrorist and other criminal communities. More and more often, human rights and dignity have to be defended against the destructive aggression of the media.

The following areas are singled out for our human rights efforts today:

- Defending human rights to the free confession of faith, prayer and worship, preservation of religious and cultural traditions, observance of religious principles in both private life and public action;
- Opposing crimes on the grounds of national and religious enmity;
- Safeguarding the individual against the arbitrary actions of those in power and employers and against violence and humiliation in his family and collective;
- Protecting life, the free choice and property of people during international, political, economic and social conflicts;
- Taking pastoral care for soldiers and protecting their rights and dignity in situations of hostilities and military service in peace time;
- Concern for the respect of the dignity and rights of those who are placed in social institutions and penitentiaries with special attention given to the disabled, orphans, the elderly and other powerless people;
- Protecting the rights of nations and ethnic groups to their own religion, language and culture;
- Concern for those whose rights, freedom and health suffer because of the actions of destructive cults;
- Supporting the family in its traditional understanding as well as fatherhood, motherhood and childhood;
- Opposing attempts to involve people in corruption and other crimes as well as in prostitution, drug addiction and gambling;
- Concern for a just economic and social order of society;
- Preventing efforts to use modern technologies and political manipulation for total control over the individual, his choice of a worldview and his private life;
- Promoting respect for law, propagating the positive experience of implementing and protecting human rights;
- Expertise of legal acts, legislative initiatives and actions by the authorities in order to prevent encroachments on human rights and dignity and aggravation of social morals.
- Participating in the public control over the law enforcement, especially in part regulating Church-State relations, and over the execution of fair court judgments.

V. 3. The human rights work of the Russian Orthodox faithful can be carried out on both the church-wide level with the blessing of the Supreme Church Authority and the level of public associations founded by lay people, as many of them are working successfully in the field of human rights already now. In her work for the protection of human rights and dignity, the Church seeks to co-operate with the State and public forces. Choosing her partners in society, the Church remembers the words that Christ the Saviour said to the apostles: 'Whoever is not against us is for us' (Mark 9:40).

V. 4. Motivated by the church teaching on human dignity, freedom and rights, Christians are called to take ethically guided social action. It can be expressed in diverse forms, such as witness before the authorities, intellectual studies, campaigns in defence of particular groups of people and their rights. Without seeking a revolutionary reconstruction of the world and acknowledging the rights of other social groups to participate in social transformations on the basis of their own worldview, the Orthodox Christians reserve the right to participate in building public life in a way that does not contradict their faith and moral principles. The Russian Orthodox Church is ready to defend the same principles in dialogue with the world community and in co-operation with people of other traditional confessions and religions.

This document is adopted by the Bishops' Council of the Russian Orthodox Church as a follow-up to her basic Social Concept. The canonical structures, clergy and laity of our Church are to be guided by this document in their socially significant statements and actions. It is to be studied in the theological schools of the Moscow Patriarchate. The document is offered to the fraternal attention of Local Orthodox Churches in the hope that it will help our churches to grow in unity and co-ordinate our practical actions. Other Christian churches and associations as well as religious communities, governmental bodies and public circles in various countries and international organisations are also invited to study and discuss it.